ENDURANCE

ENDURANCE

What It Is and How It Looks in a Believer's Life

DR. JIM HALLA

Ambassador International
GREENVILLE, SOUTH CAROLINA & BELFAST, NORTHERN IRELAND

www.ambassador-international.com

Endurance
What It Is and How It Looks in a Believer's Life

Printed in the United States of America

ISBN: 978-1-62020-025-4
eISBN: 978-1-62020-026-1

Cover Design & Page Layout by Matthew Mulder

AMBASSADOR INTERNATIONAL
Emerald House
427 Wade Hampton Blvd.
Greenville, SC 29609, USA
www.ambassador-international.com

AMBASSADOR BOOKS
The Mount
2 Woodstock Link
Belfast, BT6 8DD, Northern Ireland, UK
www.ambassador-international.com

The colophon is a trademark of Ambassador

As a former athlete I learned the value of enduring and practiced it. Enduring enabled me to make progress toward a goal. As a physcian I learned the value of enduring in graduating from medical school and during my early medical training. As a rheumatologist I have witnessed the value of enduring especially for patients with such diseases as rheumatoid arthritis. When I became a Christian, I was still enduring. However, it was when I was thrust into the arena of biblical counseling that I was able to understand endurance in a whole different light. I realized that there is enduring and that there is enduring God's way for His glory which is only true way that benefits the individual.

For me endurance took on a whole-person perspective in my own life. God gave a real fervency to refine the Biblical view of endurance and to bring His kind of enduring to the forefront of the people He graciously entrusted to me.

This book is a product of God's enduring work in me. It has bee na learning experience. Truly I have learned as I wrote. My prayer is that God will be honored and glorified as you use this book to endure His way. Blessings as you do.

Contents

Introduction

WHAT THOUGHTS COME TO MIND when you hear the word *endurance*? Do you think of the marathon runner who keeps on keeping on, the pregnant lady in labor hoping for the birth of her baby, or the kidnapped person who continues to wait and hope for rescue? Many people often express their views of endurance using such terms as "coping," "accepting," "hanging in there," "keeping on," "tolerating," "doing the best I can," and "not giving up." In my medical office, I often hear patients, when faced with various circumstances, say:

"I just take it one day at a time, hoping to get by."

"I push myself, grin and bear it just to go on, keep a smile on face, and don't give in."

"I deal with my problem daily the best I can, no matter how bad I feel."

"I just live with what I have and put up with it."

Those comments may be made in response to trouble or

pressure that God brings into one's life, because the person views the circumstance as something he doesn't like or doesn't think he deserves.

In our world, storms and ripples of life inevitably come, such as failing bodies, failing people (such as a spouse, in-laws, or boss), widowhood, mistreatment, persecution, or rejection. This list is not exhaustive, but the point is clear: trouble is never far away. People often hang in there or hold on, thinking that is the best they can do. So, they endure by "gritting their teeth," hoping, praying, and wishing for things to be different. Do you think this is what God had in mind when He called for His people to endure (John 8:31-32; 2 Timothy 2:1-7; James 1:12)? It's not.

There are at least four reasons why this kind of enduring is not how God expects believers to stay the course and run the race.

First, biblical endurance is not passive or reactive. False endurers, when asked how things are going, often say, "Nothing much has changed—same old stuff." They wait, hold on, and hang in there, hoping for circumstances to change. Their priority is "getting by." They function as if there is nothing more they can or should do. Their focus is on a change in circumstances.

Second, biblical endurance is not a matter of mere survival or protection. The driving force of enduring is a self-focused despair: "I have to survive. That's all I can do."

Third, biblical endurance is not simply duty or a badge of honor. It is not simply part of the job of living in a fallen world surrounded by flawed people. The false endurer may attempt to energize himself with the mantra of "I can't let this thing beat me or get me down. I will never give up."

Fourth, biblical endurance is not some spiritualized slogan of "I have to trust God more" or "I have to pray more." The false endurer tends to rely on his faith and prayers rather than on his God, who is in control of all things. The burden of "keeping on" is expressed as "It is tough, but what God and I are doing, with the power of prayer, is helpful," or "If it wasn't for my faith and God and the doctors, I couldn't make it," or "I just ask the Lord to help me make it through the day."

Typically, when endurance is pictured and practiced as passive/reactive, protective, dutiful, and "spiritualized," it is deceptively counterproductive to enduring God's way and dishonors God. So what is biblical endurance? Consider the victorious, abundant life that Jesus speaks about:

Then Jesus said again, "Let me assure you that I am the gate for the sheep.

All who came before me were thieves and robbers, but the sheep didn't listen to them.

> *I am the gate: anybody who comes through me will be saved*
> *and will go in and will find pasture. The only reason the*

thief comes is to steal and kill and destroy; I came so that
they may have life – in abundance!"

(John 10:7-10)

If your kind of enduring leaves you without much hope,
don't despair. God provides a clear alternative. God's kind of
endurance will motivate and allow you to reap benefits, especially in the midst of hardships. Take heart—God's word never
disappoints. Christian, you too can learn to endure God's way!
So, let's find out what God says in His Word about it.

Three words in the New Testament are translated "to endure" (See Appendix A). In contrast to the descriptions of
false endurance, each of these words conveys the truth that
the believer who practices biblical endurance is:

- Patiently, actively, and vigorously
- Carrying on and bearing up in the pressures of life
- Using biblical principles that honor God out of grati-
  tude for his salvation and sanctification

Thereby, the believer becomes more like Christ as he mod-
els the kind of endurance Jesus demonstrated during His
earthly ministry.

Scripture such as 2 Corinthians 5:9 (*So we make it our goal*
to please him, whether we are at home in the body or away from) and
Romans 8:28-29 makes clear that the goal of life is pleasing
God, that this is done by becoming more like Christ, that God
designed trouble as the context for the believer's transforma-

tion into the character of Christ, and that the believer uses what he doesn't like to develop Christlikeness.

> *And we know that in all things God works for the good of those who love him, who have been called according to his purpose. For those God foreknew he also predestined to be conformed to the likeness of his Son, that he might be the firstborn among many brothers.*
>
> (Romans 8:28-29)

Therefore, since Christlikeness is the goal for every believer and endurance is a necessary ingredient in reaching that goal, it is vitally important for us to learn what God has in mind when He tells us to endure.

CHAPTER 1

A Description of Biblical Endurance

"Lauren" and "Jesse" are college freshmen who are living far away from home. What will they do? How will each respond to the uncertainty of college life? Will they stay the course? If so, which course and how? These are endurance questions.

Bolstered by her relationship with her family and her union with Christ, Lauren presses on to be God's kind of student in an atmosphere that is anything but conducive to pleasing God. She endures through the frequent use of the means of grace, including the comfort and care of loving friends and church members and a steady diet of biblical truth offered to her by regular Bible study and meditation. She does not hide who she is in Christ.

Jesse, on the other hand, avoids any outward activity that might mark him as a Christian. He does not participate in the party scene, but neither does he openly attend church services. He wishes that he could have afforded to go to a private Christian college, but since that wasn't an option, he just has to endure where he is. He believes he can live outwardly for the Lord after he graduates, but until then, he'll endure his godless environment as best he can.

Which student is the best example of biblical endurance? The Bible's description of endurance is crucial to our understanding godly endurance. First, Scripture teaches that a person's thoughts, desires, and actions flow out of his heart (*Above all else, guard your heart, for it is the wellspring of life* [Proverbs 4:23]). As a result of man's inside-out-ness, every person simultaneously operates in a vertical and horizontal dimension. This means that one's vertical reference to life (his thoughts about and his relationship to God in Christ) at any given moment is reflected in and by horizontal interactions. Actions reflect attitudes, and behavior reflects beliefs. In other words, all of life is simultaneously theological and relational. Therefore, the external manifestations of biblical endurance must be a result of the believer's inner-man (heart) activity. A changed heart by the Holy Spirit leads the believer to desire to please God. One sign of enduring God's way is a change in *attitude* from simply getting by or getting through it to the prime motivation of pleasing God. And not only is there an attitude change, but *action* changes as well. The believer *uses* what he doesn't like (or doesn't have) to follow God's design and purpose for all believers, which is to become more like Christ. An evidence of godly endurance is the development and demonstration of the fruits of the Holy Spirit.

Second, the believer grows in the likeness of Christ *in* and *by* the pressures of life in contrast to a desire to be removed from them. Biblical endurance keeps the person on the track of developing the character of Christ. Getting the Christian out of the pressure is God's prerogative, and *using* the pressure as God's instrument to develop Christlikeness is the believer's responsibility. By the term using, I am referring to the biblical principle of taking and making an irritant into a lovely thing. We can think of this aspect of the Christian life as functioning as a Christian oyster. As the oyster takes sand and produces a pearl, so the believer uses the irritations of life to think, desire, and act like Christ. The cross comes to mind. The profound horror of the cross was transformed by Christ into the greatest good known to mankind. The believer functions as an oyster when he views irritants as God's gift to him. Instead of making relief, getting through it, and hanging on his primary goal, the believer increasingly lives more and more according to the truths of 2 Corinthians 5:9 and Romans 8:28-29 (as described above) rather than by the desire for relief. Armed with these principles and the Holy

Spirit, the believer responds to God's providential happenings in his life by developing the pearl of Christlikeness. This honors God and is best for the Christian.

These verses (Romans 8:28-29; 2 Corinthians 5:9) highlight this important truth: pleasing God is the greatest privilege and blessing that any believer has. He pleases God as he develops the character of Christ through Godly endurance, which is both the *goal* and the *means* by which the believer *grows*. Biblical endurance is given by the Holy Spirit; it is developed by the believer as he applies biblical principles to all of life (Philippians 2:12-13). To the truths taught in Romans 8:28-29 and 2 Corinthians 5:9, we must add that God's design for all believers to be like Christ was established in eternity past. In principle, this was accomplished by God placing believers "in Christ." (*For he chose us **in him** before the creation of the world to be holy and blameless in his sight* [Ephesians 1:4]).[1]

---

1   Life is relational. By that, I mean, all men live dependent on God, whether they acknowledge it or not. Only the believer is in proper relationship to God by virtue of being "in Christ." Paul expressed this relational truth with the words "in Christ" or "in him." There is an intimate fellowship and a proper union between God and man that is not physical but spiritual. It is produced and developed by the Holy Spirit through the gift of faith. The believer becomes increasingly aware of the importance of this relationship through God's Word. Being "in Christ" is the result of an instantaneous act of God whereby the person is transferred out of the family and kingdom of Satan (and self) and into the kingdom of God. He no longer lives indepen-

And it is God's design for them now.

Turning to Hebrews chapter 12, we find that the Holy Spirit teaches the same truths.

> *In your struggle against sin, you have not yet resisted to the point of shedding your blood. And you have forgotten that word of encouragement that addresses you as sons: My son, do not make light of the Lord's discipline, and do not lose heart when he rebukes you, because the Lord disciplines those he loves, and he punishes everyone he accepts as a son. Endure hardship as discipline; God is treating you as sons. For what son is not disciplined by his father? If you are not disciplined (and everyone undergoes discipline), then you are illegitimate children and not true sons. Moreover, we have all had human fathers who disciplined us and we respected them for it. How much more should we submit to the Father of our spirits and live! Our fathers disciplined us for a little while [short time] as they thought best; but God disciplines us for our good, that we may share in his holiness. No discipline seems pleasant at the time, but painful. Later on, however, it*

---

dently, but as a member of God's family. God is his Father and Christ is his Brother, but Christ is also his Lord and Master (Romans 10:9). As a result, more and more, the Christian pleases God by thinking God's thoughts, desiring God's pleasure, and obeying God out of gratitude. Pleasing God by becoming more like Christ replaces pleasing self and becomes the Christian's major motivation for biblical endurance.

> produces a harvest of righteousness and peace for those who
> have been trained by it.
>
> (Hebrews 12:4-11)

The writer of Hebrews wanted his readers to remain faithful to their calling. They were suffering hard times, and not necessarily for their own sin. As a result, some threatened to return to Judaism. What hope and motivation could he present to them to remain firm? Believers, and only believers, would faithfully, aggressively, and joyfully endure.

In these verses, the author motivated his readers to focus on one reason why God allows trouble. He emphasized that trouble, whether the consequence of one's own sin or the result of being sinned against, can be God's wise, corrective training in righteousness. A proper response to God's providential activity requires biblical endurance.[2] Therefore, the writer called his readers to be good students of God's fatherly training and loving kindness. Good students heed the Teacher's instruction in whatever form it comes by responding with joyful and thankful obedience, depending fully on His grace. These truths are summarized in 1 Corinthians 10:13.

---

2   By providence, I mean God's holy, wise, good, purposeful, and powerful preserving and governing of all His creatures and their actions for His glory and the benefit of His people (Ephesians 1:11-12; Hebrews 1:3).

> *No temptation has seized you except what is common to man. And God is faithful; he will not let you be tempted beyond what you can bear. But when you are tempted, he will also provide a way out so that you can stand up under it.*

An important truth for all believers is that God's corrective education and their biblical endurance have the *same* goal: holiness that is Christlikeness (verse 10). The author contrasts God's goal of our personal *holiness* with our all-too-common goal of personal *happiness*. Without equivocation, he states that God is in the business of making Christians holy rather than happy. He calls them to make God's goal of Christlikeness their goal (verse 7). Only in that way would they remain faithful to their calling and fulfill the goal of Christlikeness. God's providential, fatherly education and their endurance are linked.

We shall see that *both* personal discipline and biblical endurance characterized the life of Christ. So too, these are essential for believers. Remaining faithful to the goal of developing the character of Christ is accomplished by focusing on the gain rather than the pain and by focusing on the goal of pleasing God rather than on the desire for relief.

The author of the book of Hebrews knew that a commitment to God's way of enduring was needed for Christians to get victory. The same has been true for Christians throughout the ages. The commitment includes:

- **Commitment to action**: being firmly committed to God's purpose of becoming more like His Son in all situations. The believer does this by *using* trouble as God's tool to develop the character of Christ. He diligently and aggressively learns *and* applies biblical principles in order to honor God even when it seems much easier to follow his own thoughts and feelings.

- **Devotion in action**: a change in the believer's perspective about God-ordained circumstances and God's role as Teacher/Educator is essential. This will lead to an unwavering, single-minded devotion and allegiance to God, despite unpleasantness. By *using* the unpleasantness, each believer will grow in Christlikeness and remain faithful to his calling. By focusing on the gain rather than the pain, each one victoriously will pursue the character of Christ.

- **Reliance in action**: standing strong in the midst of trouble by relying on one's relationship with God in Christ, especially when there is pressure to please self, is vital as well. This is done by keeping in step with God's goal of pleasing Him.

The author of Hebrews frequently refers to Christ as the Ultimate Endurer as motivation for his readers (see 4:14-16; 6:18-20; 12:1-4). The members of the Hebrew congregation were able to endure biblically because of what they were "in Christ." Consequently, what they were and had was exceedingly "better" than anything Judaism had to offer.

Since God's goal for us is Christlikeness, becoming more like Christ is to be goal of every believer, as it was for Lauren, the college student mentioned at the beginning of this chapter. Biblical endurance is one of God's means for attaining this goal. It is the only way for the Christian to live a satisfied and contented life, and it is the preeminent way for him to glorify God. Therefore, a commitment to biblical endurance is essential for the Christian to make God's goal his goal and to endure the storms of life the way God intended.

CHAPTER 2

Foundations of Biblical Endurance

HAVING SET FORTH A DESCRIPTION of biblical endurance, let's explore its foundations by looking again at the book of Hebrews. The book is unlike the rest of the New Testament books in that the author remains unknown. Its purpose is known: it was written to Jews (Hebrews) who were beginning to suffer some persecution. Some were reconsidering their decision to put their faith in Christ. The book is both a plea and a warning to those who were threatening to apostatize by returning to Judaism as a result of growing opposition to Christianity. Some had counted the cost of change and wondered whether it was too great. They were dubious about remaining in and bearing up under the hostility associated with the name of Christ. They needed encouragement to endure the hard times.

A Vertical Reference

The author of Hebrews knew that maintaining a proper vertical reference was crucial in order to endure in a God-honoring manner. By vertical reference, I am referring to one's relationship to God. Everyone, believer and unbeliever, lives in or out of a proper relationship to God. Only the believer has a proper relationship with God because of Christ's life, death, and resurrection and the enabling work of the Holy Spirit. By His activity, the believer is enabled more and more to think, desire, and act as a God-pleaser. The author of Hebrews was fully aware that God's honor was at stake. Salvation is as much about God as it is the saved sinner. It requires a mighty work of God within the heart of the believer. The author knew his readers needed to endure biblically as a testimony to God's saving and sanctifying grace, which would glorify God and benefit them. As such, he urged his readers to focus on Christ, the Ultimate Endurer (Hebrews 12). As motivation to do so, he demonstrated how Jesus is better than Judaism, the angels, Moses, Melchizedek, Aaron, the Levitical system, and the old covenant.

Also, in Hebrews 10 through 11, he reminded his readers of the endurance of earlier saints and also their own previous endurance: *Remember those earlier days after you had received the light when you stood your ground in a great contest in the face of suffering* (Hebrews 10:32). Because of the proper vertical orientation in previous times, they had faithfully and aggressively taken hold of God's promises and applied His truth to their situation; why should they give up now?

The writer of Hebrews ended chapter 10 (verses 35-39) with a summarized thought: they needed to please God by enduring to the end.

> *So do not throw away your confidence; it will be richly rewarded. You need to persevere so that when you have done the will of God, you will receive what he has promised. For in just a little while, "he who is coming will come and will not delay, But my righteous one will live by faith. And if he shrinks back, I will not be pleased with him." But we are not of those who shrink back and are destroyed, but of those who believe and are saved.*
>
> (Hebrews 10:35-39)

In chapter 11, he reminds them of the Old Testament saints whose lives were characterized by godly, faithful endurance. They had fought the good fight of faith, choosing to remain true to God in difficult situations. And they had won! They were winners in and through Christ (Romans 8:35-37). Powerfully, the author closed the chapter (verses 39-40) by saying that biblical endurers, even though they have not yet laid hold of what God has promised, are motivated by something better: that which awaits them in the future.

> *These were all commended for their faith, yet none of them received what had been promised. God had planned something better for us so that only together with us would they be made perfect.*

(Hebrews 11:39-40)

An Eternal Perspective

The saints mentioned in chapters 10 and 11 were able to practice God-honoring endurance because they lived with an eternal perspective (Hebrews 11:39-40). They looked beyond their pain and unpleasantness to the gain: the eternal joy of perfected living in God's presence. As faithful witnesses of God's grace, they found that holding on to this life and its "things" were less important. They lived with an eternal gaze, faithfully responding to hardships and even death itself. Their God-ward, eternal focus enabled them to control not only their actions, but even their thoughts and desires (Philippians 3:12-15; Colossians 3:1-3).[3]

---

3   Having been freed from the bondage and power of sin, all believers are able to, and will, "faithfully endure to the end" (John 8:31-36). The author of Hebrews knew well that active, aggressive, faithful living as a God-pleaser required God-honoring endurance that required saving faith. Saving faith is an informed, intelligent faith that focuses on Jesus Christ (John 14:6). The Hebrew believers were to continue

A Good God's Control

In Hebrews 12:1-4, the author further encouraged his readers to endure biblically because God providentially controls all things for His purpose. Among other things, God's purpose always includes bringing about His glory and the good of His people (12:1). He actively works in history to see that His plan is carried out.

> *Therefore, since we are surrounded by such a great cloud of witnesses, let us throw off everything that hinders and the sin that so easily entangles, and let us run with perseverance the race marked out for us. Let us fix our eyes on Jesus, the author and perfecter of our faith, who for the joy set before   him endured the cross, scorning its shame, and sat down at the right hand of the throne of God. Consider him who endured such opposition from sinful men, so that you will not grow weary and lose heart. In your struggle against sin, you have not yet resisted to the point of shedding your blood.*
>
> (Hebrews 12:1-4)

Faced with tough times, it was easy for the believers to focus on what people were doing to them and their own at-

---

to evaluate and respond to life through the eyes of saving faith (see Hebrews 10 and 11). They had not depended on "sensual living" (interpreting circumstances through the physical senses of sight, touch, taste, or smell) for motivation, direction, and encouragement.

tempts to control things. The writer of Hebrews knew appearances deceive. Never minimizing trouble, he reminded his readers of God's presence, provisions, power, and purpose. Contrary to feelings, surely God was in control and energetically working all things according to the counsel of His will (Romans 8:28-29; Ephesians 1:11-12).

Suprasensual Living

Rather than emphasizing the unpleasantness of the circumstances, the saints in Hebrews 10-11 focused on the God of those circumstances. They were biblical endurers who lived "beyond their senses." That is, they lived suprasensually, evaluating life through the grid of biblical truth rather than through circumstances, their reasoning, or feelings. Viewing the storms and ripples of life through the eyes of saving faith enabled them to "see" Jesus, the Author and Completer of their faith and the Ultimate Endurer, their model: *Let us fix our eyes on Jesus, the Author and Perfecter of our faith, who for the joy set before him endured the cross, scorning its shame, and sat down at the right hand of the throne of God* (Hebrews 12:2). The word translated "fix" means to focus the mind in an effort to reach the goal, to look intently, giving full attention to a distant object. Here, in this verse, the object in view is Jesus Himself. Suprasensual living involves a Christ-centered focus for evaluating and responding to God's providence.

In Scripture, two people walked on water: Jesus and Peter

(Matthew 14:22-33). Peter failed to sustain his walk once he took his eyes off Jesus and chose instead to focus on the stormy waves and his impotence. Yet, his focus quickly returned to Christ as he began to sink beneath the waves. In contrast, in 1 Samuel 17, David focused on Jehovah rather than Goliath. As a result, he rushed into battle with God's victory in sight. And God won through David! David's focus is an example of biblical "eye-fixing." John, in 1 John 3:1-3, taught the same truth.

Moreover, suprasensual living characterized Jesus' life:

> *Meanwhile his disciples urged him, "Rabbi, eat something." But he said to them, "I have food to eat that you know nothing about." Then his disciples said to each other, "Could someone have brought him food?" "My food," said Jesus, "is to do the will of him who sent me and finish his work."*
>
> (John 4:31-34)

Saints of all ages have exercised their capacity for suprasensual living. Like the Old Testament heroes of Hebrews 10 and 11, Christians today are able to evaluate life suprasensually since God has provided the power, the purpose, the plan, the promises, and the provisions in order to respond to life God's way. Biblical endurance comes from victoriously pursuing Christlikeness.

The Race

Contrary to popular thinking (as emphasized by the culture's description of non-godly endurance), life is not a "rat race." Nor is it to be lived out of a survival mentality. Biblically, life is a struggle, a race. Unfortunately, too many Christians fail to acknowledge this truth and thus fail to compete with endurance. In the original language, the word translated as "race" is *agon,* a term that comes over into English as "agony." In the New Testament, it is translated as "race" and "struggle," indicating that effort and hard work are involved. The words taken from the Greek athletic world picture running, boxing, and wrestling. In Hebrews, the author described his readers' situation that shows:[4]

1. Each person is in the race, and getting out is impossible;

---

4   The term is used in the noun form six times: Hebrews 12:1; 1 Timothy 6:12; 2 Timothy 4:7; Philippians 1:30; Colossians 2:1; 1 Thessalonians 2:2. The verb form *agonizomai* is used seven times: 1 Corinthians 9:25; John 18:36; 1 Timothy 6:12; 2 Timothy 4:7; Luke 13:24; Colossians 1:29; 4:12. Hebrews 12:4 translates "struggle" using *antagonizomai,* a compound word (*anti* and *agonizomai*), which means to be in conflict with and is used only once in the New Testament. Also, Paul makes use of the boxing metaphor in 1 Corinthians 9:24-27. The Corinthians were familiar with the goal and the "how" of running. Endurance and self-control were indispensable for running and winning the race God's way.

2. There are rules and regulations to observe in competing;

3. There is a starting point and a finishing point;

4. Running the race and fighting the good fight is costly—it requires effort;

5. Each person must prepare in order to successfully participate;

6. There is a prize to be won—victory comes as the believer grows and learns godly endurance.

In Hebrews 12:1, the author pointed back to the multitude of faithfully-enduring saints to accentuate the fact that his readers had the same God, were in the same God-designed race, and, like them, could be victorious. Biblical truth never minimizes the difficulties of living in a fallen world with sin-cursed bodies, but instead always maximizes God's grace and resources. Since you are in the race, Christian, how well are you running?

Because God providentially placed you, and every Christian, in "the race," He expects you and them to honor Him 24/7 by becoming more like Christ. This includes responding to trouble God's way by thinking, desiring, and acting as a God-pleaser. Habitual living as a God-pleaser patterned after Christ and His Word is enduring biblically. Biblical endurance enables you to remain in your situation irrespective of the pressure by functioning as a Christian oyster.

The best way to achieve Christian growth is by knowing what you are in Christ—its costs to Christ and to you the believer, and its benefits—and acting accordingly. God graciously equips His people to please Him through consistent faithfulness and hopefulness, thereby fulfilling God's design determined in eternity past (Ephesians 1:4). How do you respond to hard times? Do you need help? As you can see, God doesn't leave you in doubt as to how to be victorious. He expects you to stand firm, stay true in the midst of trouble, and loyally please Him. This is no casual matter. The call to endurance is common throughout the New Testament. Peter and Paul exhorted their readers to endure by remaining true to their calling and election (Ephesians 4:1-3; Philippians 2:12-13; 2 Peter 1:10).

The author of Hebrews knew that because people function from the inside out, his readers were in a life-and-death struggle which involved choosing between God-honoring endurance (which enabled them to complete the race as God-pleasers) or going back to their former, hopeless ways of self-pleasing (which means never finishing the race). The struggle they faced included the continuing habits formed in Satan's family and kingdom, where self-pleasing took center stage.

God's child, though radically changed and transferred into God's kingdom and family, still has the tendency to please himself. But God's grace, enabling him to faithfully endure, is at his disposal. As demonstrated by these Old Testament saints, the only way to successfully run the race of life and finish as a victor is by God-honoring endurance. James makes the same point: *Blessed is the man who perseveres under trial, because when he has stood the test, he will receive the crown of life that God has promised to those who love him* (James 1:12).

Biblical "Eye-Fixing"

Another key for enduring biblically is a proper focus. The writer of Hebrews told his people that as they ran the grueling race set before them, they must fix their eyes on Jesus Christ (Hebrews 12:2). As is suprasensual living, "biblical eye-fixing" is having a Christ-centered focus. Paul expressed the same truth in Colossians 3:1-3.

> *Since, then, you have been raised with Christ, set your hearts on the things above, where Christ is seated at the right hand of God. Set your mind on things above, not on earthly things. For you died, and your life is now hidden with Christ in God.*
>
> (Colossians 3:1-3)

Paul called the Colossians to "right mindedness," i.e., proper thinking. They had the mind of Christ—that is, the indwelling Holy Spirit who enabled them to think God's thoughts after Him (1 Corinthians 2:16). They were able to think in a biblically-controlled manner. Being right minded means giving loyalty, allegiance, affection, and devotion to Christ rather than to self. It means focusing on pleasing God, especially when it is easier to please self. Jesus demonstrated such right mindedness throughout His life (see John 4:31-34). Paul's right mindedness enabled him to actively, energetically, and purposefully endure hard times God's way. He had a good God to please and a ministry to complete (2 Corinthians 4:1, 16-18; Philippians 1:19-21). He had no "rat race" mentality. God's children are more than rats!

Furthermore, according to Colossians, the things above (literally, "upward things") are the ascended Christ of glory and the Christian's relationship with Him. Paul tells the Colossians to pattern their life after Christ. The Christian does that by putting off the "I wantsies" and, among other things, putting on biblical endurance and the characteristics of Christ mentioned in verses 12 through 13 of chapter 3 (compassion, kindness, humility, gentleness, patience, bearing with and forgiving one another, and love)—in other words, rejecting one's natural, selfish tendencies to live a life that pleases God. Union and fellowship with Christ should daily impact how the Christian lives. It did for Paul (Philippians 3:3-11; Galatians 2:20), and it should for you.

The apostle John taught the same eye-fixing truth as hope:

> *How great is the love the Father has lavished on us, that we should be called children of God! And that is what we are! The reason the world does not know us is that it did not know him. Dear friends, now we are children of God, and what we will be has not yet been made known. But we know that when he appears, we shall be like him, for we shall see him as he is. Everyone who has this hope in him purifies himself, just as he is pure.*

(1 John 3:1-3)

John reminded his readers of the awesomeness of God's Fatherhood. As part of God's family, the child of God has Jesus as his brother and expects to see Him personally in heaven (Matthew 28:10; Hebrews 2:10-12). This is the ultimate promise given to every believer (see Hebrews 11:39-40). As good as it is to be God's child and to grow in Christlikeness, being in the eternal presence of God is far superior. Clearly, biblical endurance is goal-oriented: growing Christlikeness now, and the certain hope of living face-to-face with God, having become as completely righteous and holy as Jesus Himself.

Relationships matter: you are not alone

Returning to Hebrews 12, the writer gave the ultimate foundation for endurance: the believer's relationship with

Christ. Jesus, who had the proper perspective on life, was the Ultimate Endurer (verse 2). He is the Source, Giver, and Object of saving, enabling grace and enduring faith. He is not some abstract force, but a person who endured. He completely identified with humankind (you) by running the race that you are in (Hebrews 4:14-16). Jesus came to please His Father (John 4:31-34). Nothing deterred Him from that. Pleasing God was His motivation. So when we say Jesus ran the race, it means He lived as the perfect man; He accomplished what Adam was designed to do pre-Fall. Adam was faced with an allegiance and devotion issue: to please himself or please God by obedience. So, Jesus too was tempted to get out of the race. But He ran to win, and He did! He is the true Victor. As a result, you must pattern your endurance after Him (James 1:12).

Paul understood these facts and under the direction of the Holy Spirit wrote:

> *Who shall separate us from the love of Christ? Shall trouble or hardship or persecution or famine or nakedness or danger or sword? As it is written: "For your sake we face death all day along; we are considered as sheep to be slaughtered." No, in all these things, we are more than conquerors through him who loved us. For I am convinced that neither death nor life, neither angels nor demons, neither the present nor the future, nor any powers, neither height nor depth, nor anything else in all creation, will be*

*able to separate us from the love of God that is in Christ
Jesus our Lord.*

(Romans 8:35-39)

Every Christian has been graced by God (both saving and
enabling grace) and should function as more than a con-
queror as he faithfully endures—out of gratitude for the Cross.
Rather than simply hanging in or hanging on, he can view all
trouble as an opportunity, even an adventure, to please God.
He does that by responding to circumstances with his eyes
off self and the circumstances. Instead, his focus is on Christ,
the promises of God, and the goal of becoming more like his
Savior. He reaches that goal only through purposeful, biblical
endurance that enables him to use trouble to become more
like Christ (Romans 5:1-5; 1 Peter 1:6-7; James 1:2-4). That
is God's way!

CHAPTER 3

Characteristics of Biblical Endurance

IN THIS CHAPTER I LAY out a number of characteristics of God-honoring endurance gleaned from Scripture. The short discussion of each is intended to provide further insight into what it means to endure biblically.

1. Biblical endurance is the learned expression of an inward reality of a person's changed heart:

> *May the Lord direct your hearts into God's love and into Christ's patience*
>
> (2 Thessalonians 3:5).

In his closing prayer for the beloved at Thessalonica, Paul emphasized the inward element of godly endurance. He encouraged the people by reminding them that endurance was characteristic of Christ while on earth and that it should characterize them—and it did!

Paul drew a connection between God's love and our endurance. Elsewhere, Paul teaches that biblical love endures, and godly endurance is God and other-motivated. The lover never gives up, and the endurer never stops loving (1 Corinthians 13:4-7). The Christian endures because he has first been loved by God (1 John 4:19). He grows in his love for God out of gratitude for the Cross. He remains fixed on God's purpose in the situation rather than self-interest and on finding relief (2 Corinthians 5:14-15). There is a connection between love and endurance because God is the source of both (1 John 4:8; Romans 5:3-5; 15:4).

Biblical endurance begins in the heart and leads to Christlikeness *in* and *by* the pressure, not *out* of it. The enduring Christian maintains a proper vertical reference, focusing on what God is doing and what God expects him to do. The biblical endure has a view of a big God and a small self. He stays the course; his desire to get out is always checked by a greater desire to please God. Therefore, he is compassionate and tenderhearted, serves to the degree that he can, and practices self-control.

As one example, consider "Barbara," a widow who supports herself, has a church family, and who has questions about where she is, where she is to go, and how she is to get there. She loves the Lord but finds herself caught up in the comings and goings of ordinary life. She faces waking up in the morning, seeing only the cat, going to work, and facing only the grumbles and complaints of both colleagues and clients. What does she do, not only this morning, but every morning and every evening? In fact, what does she do, think, and desire 24/7? She could respond to God's providence sensually. If that's her choice, then getting by, coping, and trying to survive can easily become her modus operandi for life. If she chooses that approach, self takes center stage, and her relationship to Christ has little functional value in the ordinary activities of life. Some people may call this enduring, but certainly it is a non-God-honoring activity. Rather, the godly endurer that Barbara has become filters all of life, including God's providence to her personally, vertically, and that controls her horizontal reference and relationships to and in life. Therefore, she makes use of the means of grace (personal prayer, Bible reading, and meditation) and looks to comfort others rather than to be comforted. She is an encourager rather than seeking to be encouraged. She is a lover rather than seeking to be loved. In short, she endures in a God-honoring way by using pressures in her life to grow and become more like Christ.

In one sense, God is "on trial" in the life of every Christian because God places Himself in that position. In Psalm 34:8 (*Taste and see that the Lord is good; blessed is the man who takes refuge in him*), God bids His people to come and experience His *Godness*, which includes His goodness (Exodus 33:19). Moreover, in the book of Job, we find Satan in God's presence, challenging God (1:9-11; 2:4-6). He represents God as endorsing the "health and wealth" prosperity gospel that is so prevalent today. Satan claimed: "God, you aren't really that good. You have provided for Job and have him in your back pocket. When problems come, he will curse you, and then the world will know that you both are counterfeit." God's response was something like this: "I Am Who I Am. Therefore, I authorize you to be My agent to test your accusations. Job will come out of the refiner's fire truly prosperous and proving Me the Victor." The book chronicles Job's hard times and—to him—the seemingly purpose-less onslaught to him, his possessions, and his family. He faithfully endured, although he sinned along the way. His endurance led him to a fuller understanding of who God is and who Job himself was (see Job 42:1-6). In the end, God had Job pray for his friends. It was only after Job repented and mediated on behalf of his friends that God restored his physical fortune. Job got it right!

2. The manifestations of biblical endurance are *visible* and *worthy of praise*:

> *We ought always to thank God for you, brothers, and rightly so, because your faith is growing more and more, and the love every one of you has for each other is increasing. Therefore among God's churches we boast about your perseverance and faith in all your persecutions and trials that you are enduring.*
>
> (2 Thessalonians 1:3-4)

Godly endurance is to be plainly visible among men. It is observable. The biblical endurer stands out as a light in darkness or a beacon on a vast ocean. It is more than a state of mind or mere faith. It is more than coping or hanging in there. It is not simply being present in the situation. It embraces a proper vertical reference and is motivated by the desire to please God. It is using tough times as one's classroom to grow by grace (2 Peter 3:18). In Thessalonica, God's work in the hearts of the people was visibly apparent as a testimony to God's divine regenerating and sanctifying grace (also see 1 Thessalonians 1:2-3; Hebrews 12:11; 2 Peter 1:5-10; Luke 8:15). By their endurance—expressed by their faith, love, and hope—the saints at Thessalonica were known by the world as changed people.

Both Paul and the author of Hebrews linked godly endurance and saving faith. Most Christians will readily admit that they haven't arrived in terms of Christlikeness, but the idea that their faith needs refining is less accepted. For these dear people, godly endurance may be lacking.

3. Biblical endurance is joyfully and hopefully *purposeful*:

> *Therefore since you have been justified through faith, we have peace with God through our Lord Jesus Christ, through whom we have gained access by faith into this grace in which we now stand. And we rejoice in the hope of the glory of God. Not only so, but also rejoice in our sufferings because we know that suffering produces perseverance; perseverance, character; and character, hope. And we know that hope does not disappoint us, because God has poured*

*out His love into our hearts by the Holy Spirit, whom
was given us.*

(Romans 5:1-5)

*Consider it pure joy, my brothers, when you face trials
of many kinds because you know the testing of your faith
develops perseverance. Perseverance must finish its work
so that you may be mature and complete, not lacking
anything.*

(James 1:2-4)

*No temptation has seized you except what is common to
man. And God is faithful; he will not let you be tempted
beyond what you can bear. But when you are tempted,
he will also provide a way out so that you can stand up
under it.*

(1 Corinthians 10:13)

As a result of his salvation, the Christian is the most changed
person. He demonstrates a transformation not possible for the
unbeliever. God transferred him from the kingdom of Satan,
where "me first" and "I want" are the standard for living, to
the kingdom of God; as such, the believer changes his self-
focus to pleasing God out of gratitude for His salvation. He
knows he is not a victim to *and* in his circumstances. Therefore,
he is able to joyfully acknowledge, accept, and act upon the
fact that a good, purposeful God is at work in his life. Biblical

endurance requires *and* produces this attitude and activity. It enables him to become more like Christ as he makes God's goal his goal. He puts on the character of Christ rather than "holding on," coping, or tolerating.

In Romans 5:1-5, Paul teaches that a believer's right standing before God results in peace with God.[5] The knowledge of this change in judicial standing and acceptance before God has far-reaching effects. The believer can view and respond to trouble in a radically different way. He rejoices in trouble (1 Peter 1:6-7). This may seem rather morbid except for the fact that Paul knew trouble always had a purpose in God's plan. A right response to it produces—and requires—godly endurance. And godly endurance always results in proven and genuine trustworthiness that is a testimony to God's grace and the believer's changed heart. Growing trustworthiness and trustfulness come through knowing and doing what is required in Scripture.

Paul completes his sequence of thought by pointing to hope. Hope and endurance go hand in hand. True hope never disappoints; neither does biblical endurance. Biblical hope is the confident expectation that God is the true Promise

---

5   The doctrine of justification (by faith) can be defined as an act of God's free grace by which He pardons and declares the believer not guilty, accepting him as righteous in His sight due to Christ's perfect life and perfect death that God has counted as the believer's.

Maker and Keeper. God means what He says and does what He means. He can be trusted! As a result, the believer endures purposefully, which enables him to reach the finish line. God doesn't give up, so why should you? What ought to be the hope of every child of God? It is to know and act upon the fact that God is his Father and to bask in the thought that one day God will say, "Well done, good and faithful servant! ...Come and share your master's gladness" (Matthew 25:21, 23).

James teaches the same truths (James 1:2-4). In this passage, he begins by urging right thinking. (The word in the original language has within it the idea of leading oneself to think a certain way.) James knew that biblically-controlled thinking in the midst of trouble was not a natural response. The way that the believer is to think about trouble is in marked contrast to the mindset of the culture. The joy in the troubles (trials) is not because of unpleasantness but God's purpose for them. The end result of troubles rightly responded to is a mature Christian through proven genuineness.

Both Paul and James knew that trouble was God's refining fire, the purpose of which was to remove the dross (impurities) from one's faith. And yet consider this statement: "If it wasn't for my faith, and God, I wouldn't be able to keep going." The idea that "my faith" needs "fixing" (refining and purifying) seems foreign and even repugnant to many Christians. These dear children of God have missed the point. The issue is not the size of a person's faith. In Matthew's Gospel, Jesus said to the disciples at least four times: "O you of little faith" (8:30; 8:26; 14:31; 16:8). In each case, the issue was not the *fact* of their faith, but their faithfulness. Faith is a gift, and God, the Giver of faith, doesn't give poor gifts. God expects and deserves right use of His gifts. God is trustworthy; the cross and the resurrection prove that fact (Ephesians 2:8-9; James 1:17). Therefore, for every believer in any situation, the call is for him to faithfully endure.

Both Paul and James teach that biblical endurance is not simply duty. Rather, it is staying in the situation God's way for His glory and the believer's benefit. The theme that trouble is intended to be purposeful runs throughout Scripture (consider such passages as Psalm 119:65-71; Isaiah 38:15-17; Romans 5:1-5; 2 Corinthians 12:7-10; James 1:2-4; 1 Peter 1:6-7). It was not the hardship itself that motivated the believer to rejoice, but the benefits of handling trouble God's way. Some of those benefits include a maturing and deepening *reliance* on a very big God, an increasing *thankfulness* for God's provisions, a growing *contentment* in the face of hardship, and an increasing *understanding* that God works all things for His glory and the Christian's benefit (Romans 8:28-29). As I have mentioned, staying in the situation God's way produces biblical endurance as well as requires it. Paul captures this thought in Philippians 4:13: *I can do all things through Him who gives me strength.* "All things" is specific: it is pleasing God in thought, desire, and deed (even when you don't feel like it), and believing that the storms of life are not bigger than God. In contrast, self-pleasing focuses on the unpleasantness of the situation and relief *from* it rather than on victory *in* the trouble (see footnote 11).

Clearly, Scripture teaches that you need to grow as a faithful person. To help you assess where you are in this area, ask yourself: is God worthy and deserving of your trust at the moment of your pressure? Are you a God-trusting person in the trouble? Scripture teaches and the Cross proves that God is trustworthy, and you are to be growing as a trusting person. God will sustain you as you faithfully and joyfully endure by exercising His gift of faith daily.

4. Biblical endurance is *hope engendering:*

> *Not only so, but we ourselves, who have the first fruits of the Spirit, the creation, groan inwardly as we wait eagerly for our adoption as sons, the redemption of our bodies. For in this hope we were saved. But hope that is seen is no hope at all. Who hopes for what he already has? But if we hope for what we do not yet have, we wait for it patiently.*
>
> (Romans 8:23-25)

> *We continually remember before our God and Father your work produced by faith, your labor prompted by love,*

and your endurance inspired by hope in Our Lord Jesus
Christ.

(1 Thessalonians 1:3)

True biblical hope is the *expectation* of fulfillment of God's promises. It is characterized by patient and aggressive waiting for what we do not see and requires suprasensual living. Moreover, it is a personal attitude of a confident, sure expectation of something *good* because God makes and keeps promises, and you are the recipient of them. This definition contrasts with false hope, which is a hope-so hope based on sensual living that looks for relief and changed circumstances. Acting on God's promises requires biblical endurance *and* is enduring God's way. The believer knows that he is in the race, that he will finish, and that God will reward him accordingly (James 1:12).

In Romans 8, Paul spoke of hard times. Creation groans, and so do God's people (8:18-25). Those at Rome did not see or feel evidence of bodily redemption. In fact, unlike most Christians today in the Western world, they experienced just the opposite: persecution and death. In the midst of their trouble, they could lose their course and end in despair. Their bodily redemption, though promised, was not yet realized. In verse 24, Paul wrote that salvation was not simply the forgiveness of sins, but the assurance of eternal life and ultimate freedom from the bondage of sin's power and suffering—its misery.

Paul pointed them away from what they could see and feel to the greater reality of the promise of eternal life and complete redemption. He called them to a proper vertical reference, an eternal perspective, and suprasensual living.

The biblical endurer pleases God by staying focused on God's promises. And he wins—as Christ did! The Christian knows and acts upon these facts: God is God, He gives concrete direction in Scripture for addressing all of life, and He has promised victory in His Son, guaranteed by the indwelling Holy Spirit. That victory is being fulfilled now as people are saved, and saved people endure to the end. As a new creature in Christ, the Christian, united to Christ and having the indwelling Holy Spirit, has a foretaste of heavenly things. Therefore, hope motivates him to endure and to live knowing that God is who He says He is: the true Promise Keeper. He doesn't desert His people.

Summarizing the section, godly endurance requires hope, and hopeful living requires endurance (1 Thessalonians 1:3). Both are essential for successfully running the race, fighting the good fight, and disciplining self for godliness (Hebrews 12:1-4; 1 Timothy 6:12; 2 Timothy 4:7). Therefore, enduring in a biblical fashion is not some flimsy, paltry sense of holding on, trying to get by, coping, or accepting. Rather, it is essential in moving you toward the final fulfillment of God's original design: to become more like Christ (Ephesians 1:4; 5:26-27).

Endurance enables you to think as a victor because you are able to use what you don't like to grow into one. That is one of the lessons of the Cross.

5. Biblical endurance is *refreshingly knowledgeable*:

> *For everything that was written in the past was written to teach us, so that through the endurance and the encouragement of the Scriptures we might have hope.*
>
> (Romans 15:4)

One purpose of all Scripture, both Old and New Testaments, is to inform God's people what life is about and how to get victory (2 Peter 1:3-4; Titus 1:1). This includes what to think and how to relate to life, self, others, and God. Part of the basis for right thinking includes God's victory in His Son, His faithfulness in providing His Spirit, and the eternal destiny that awaits all of God's people. In this verse, Paul teaches that endurance, encouragement, and hope come through Scripture, which results in victory. Since hope is grounded in knowing God's promises and acting on His trustworthiness, God expects His people to be informed and knowledgeable.

Endurance does not come apart from a growing understanding of Scripture. Since Scripture is God's truth and the believer's owner's manual for life, it is all the believer needs for living a satisfied and contented life. Biblically-controlled thinking and its application is the key to biblical endurance and a truly, victorious life.

Elsewhere, Paul drew a connection between trouble, endurance, and hope (1 Thessalonians 1:3). In our passage, he added to that trio, knowledge through the Scripture and the Holy Spirit. Paul wrote elsewhere that Scripture has its origin in God; therefore it is God's clear, authoritative, and sufficient truth that fully equips the Christian for godly living (2 Timothy 3:16-17). Moreover, God sent another Encourager of the same kind as Jesus Christ: His Holy Spirit (John 15:26-27; 16:13). The Spirit applies God's truth and enlightens the mind of every believer. Otherwise, self would rule, and each one would do what is right in his own eyes, trusting himself rather than the unchangeable Word of God (Judges 17:6; 21:25; Proverbs 3:5-8). The faithful Christian is refreshingly content and confident, and his life is simplified as he relies more and more on the Word of God for direction and solving problems. He takes refuge not in relief, escape, or self, but in God (Psalm 18:1-3; 46:1-3).

6. Biblical endurance is *intimately comforting*:

> *Praise be to the God and Father of our Lord Jesus Christ, the Father of compassion and God of all comfort, who comforts us in all our troubles so that we can comfort those in any trouble with the comfort that we ourselves received from God. For just as the sufferings of Christ flow over into our lives so also through Christ our comfort overflows.*

If we are distressed, it is for your comfort and salvation; if we are comforted, it is for your comfort which produces in you patient endurance of the same sufferings we suffer. Indeed, in our hearts we felt the sentence of death. But this happened that we might not rely on ourselves but on God who raises the dead.

(2 Corinthians 1:3-6, 9)

In verses 3-4, Paul pointed to the true Source of all help and comfort: God. The believer is the most comforted person through his restored relationship with God in Christ. His guilt and condemnation have been taken by Christ. He is forgiven, redeemed, delivered, and brought into a proper relationship with Him. That is true comfort! But Paul knew that in the midst of trouble, it was easy to seek false comfort. In preparation for those times, every Christian must invest himself more and more in understanding who Jesus is and what the Christian is "in Christ" (Philippians 3:7-11). A growing knowledge of what it cost God and Jesus for the believer's union with Christ and of its benefits are powerful motivators for enduring God's way. That investment produces a greater submission to God's purpose in trouble, thereby simplifying life, which leads to satisfaction and contentment (Matthew 11:28-30).

One benefit of receiving God's comfort for the Christian is enduring trouble by applying biblical principles appropriate to his situation. Trouble is one of God's instruments for learning, receiving, and experiencing God's comfort. Therefore, the believer is able to endure more faithfully. That is comfort!

Being comforted leads to a second benefit of enduring God's way. The biblical endurer is one who has been comforted and, in response, develops as both a comforter and comfortee. God expects those who have received his comfort to gratefully comfort others. Paul's response to trouble commended him to the Corinthian saints as God's servant and was a sign of his apostolic calling (2 Corinthians 6:4; 12:12). Today, since there are no apostles, he who endures God's way is a testimony of gratitude for God's graciousness.

A third benefit of being comforted by God is a maturing trust and reliance on God and His promises. As the believer endures God's way, he comforts others in the same way that he has been comforted.

Furthermore, in verse 9, Paul wrote that God ordains trouble in order to turn the believer away from self and his own resources and toward God and His resources. Paul wrote that he was moved from self-reliance to trust in God. He desired the same continuing and maturing change for the Corinthian saints. He knew that they had been wonderfully comforted at salvation and that God had and would continue to sustain them until He called them home. As the most comforted people, the saints at Corinth were to comfort others. Having the same experience is not necessary

to comfort others. Rather, the key to comforting others is
a reliance on the God of circumstances and His help. As a
result, the comforted believer, irrespective of the affliction,
can minister to anyone in need.

7. Biblical endurance is to be *powerfully joyful:*

> *Being strengthened with all power according to his glorious*
> *might so that you may have great endurance and patience,*
> *and joyfully giving thanks to the Father, who qualified*
> *you to share in the inheritance of the saints in the kingdom*
> *of light.*

(Colossians 1:11-12)

The enduring saint will be joyful as he develops God's
way of enduring (2 Corinthians 4:16; Ephesians 3:16). The
end product of godly endurance is a mature, purified, joyful faith. Joy comes in the midst of trouble and *not* because
of trouble itself (John 15:11; 16:20-22; James 1:2-4). The
key is your response to it. As we have seen in Jesus' cross-
centered life and death, joy is not necessarily relief. Rather,
it is functioning as a God-pleaser using irritants (the cross,
in Jesus' case) in order to please God. The joy of pleasing
God is available to you here on this earth, and it will be
fully realized in heaven.

Joy is not the same as happiness. Happiness depends on
happenings. It is determined by that which is outside of
a person. It looks at self and circumstances, is temporary,

and is never commanded in Scripture. In contrast, joy is commanded; it looks away from self and to God. Paul was no stranger to the hardness of life, and he rejoiced in the Lord (Romans 5:1-5; 2 Corinthians 1:8-10; 4:7-12; 11:23-28). One antidote for the Philippians and their problem of disunity was to rejoice in the Lord by centering on the goal of pleasing Him (Philippians 3:1; 4:4). An expression of pleasing God would be for the Philippian saints to consider others more important than themselves (Philippians 2:3-4). This required the mind of Christ (Philippians 2:5).

8. Biblical endurance is *desirable* and *to be pursued*:

> *But you, man of God, flee these things; pursue righteousness,*
> *godliness, faithfulness, love, endurance, meekness.*
>
> (1Timothy 6:11)

The child of God learns and develops endurance; it is also a fruit of the Spirit. 6 Endurance doesn't come about apart from the Spirit, but neither is it zapped into the believer. The Spirit produces His fruits, but the believer diligently and earnestly pursues them as a hound tracking its prey (1 Timothy 6:11; 2 Timothy 2:22). Endurance is required for fighting the gallant fight of faith and for self-

---

6   Galatians 5:22: the word translated "patience" is *macrothumia,* which typically refers to patient tolerance of people rather than things. See appendix A.

discipline (2 Timothy 4:7; 1 Timothy 6:12).

9. Biblical endurance demands *faithful commitment*:

> *Endure hardship with us like a good soldier of Christ Jesus. No one serving as a soldier gets involved in civilian affairs – he wants to please his commanding officer. Similarly, if anyone competes as an athlete, he doesn't receive the victor's crown unless he competes according to the rules. The hardworking farmer should be the first to receive a share of the crops. Reflect on what I am saying, for the Lord will give you insight into all this.*

(2 Timothy 2:4-7)

Paul reminded Timothy that a "war" is going on and that endurance is both commanded and required in order to win. Paul called for full commitment to the war effort. There was to be no divided allegiance. The war included an attack on God's name and on His people. That includes you! Both as a child of the King and minister of the gospel, trouble pursued Timothy, which is why Paul called Timothy (and calls you) to remain firm and faithful (2 Timothy 2:3-13; 3:12; also see 1 Peter 1:6-8; James 1:2-4; John 15:18-20). Paul always remembered God's faithfulness to him and all the saints. The idea of being forgotten by God has no place in the Christian's thinking (1 Corinthians 10:13).[7]

---

7   In this verse, there are at least four promises, one of which is that God is faithful to His promises and to His people. The trustworthiness of

Paul knew that suffering and trouble were the platforms upon which Timothy was called to endure. His endurance was required to faithfully represent God and to truthfully present the gospel. Paul motivated Timothy to fight the good fight by emphasizing hopeful endurance and the comfort that comes from it.

In verses 3-7 of 2 Timothy, Paul spelled out how endurance would look and how it was to be developed. He used the example of a soldier who wished to please his commander-in-chief (verse 4). If the soldier was preoccupied with non-military affairs, his allegiance would be divided. Rather, the soldier must endure in his task of pleasing his chief by leaving other business matters at home. Similarly in verse 5, Paul used the example of an athlete who tried to compete in a contest by his own rules. As a consequence of his lack of allegiance, he didn't endure to the end and didn't receive the winner's wreath. In verse 6, we read of an enduring farmer who was diligently focused on his task and was rewarded.

Paul knew these truths may be hard to apply, so, on cue, he penned verse 7. He pointed to God's gift of understand-

---

God can never be doubted, and this fact breeds confidence and hope. You are not alone, because your separation from God has been dealt with at the cross. The issue is never your aloneness or God's lack of faithfulness, but you functioning as a trusting person. And since every Christian has the capacity for hopeful trust, you can and will develop as a God-truster.

ing. Paul knew that an enduringly faithful commitment to Christ requires truth. Timothy was to think hard and often about the race set before him (Hebrews 12:1-4). Timothy's struggles were never to be considered apart from who Christ was, what He did, and what Timothy was called to do.

Biblical endurance demands that you "own" your personal relationship with Christ. The enduring saint is so impacted by being "in Christ" that he faithfully and joyfully endures to the end. Knowledgeable endurance helps produce faithful endurance. Being in the presence of God is an end-product of suprasensual living, biblical eye-fixing, and an eternal perspective of life. These perspectives motivate the believer to endure God's way. Christ endured for the honor of His Father. He knew what He was doing. So too it should be for saints in all ages. They know that God's purpose and their good are inextricably linked and will be complete when Jesus returns.

10. Biblical endurance is *goal oriented* and *vertically referenced*:

> *Remember Jesus Christ, raised from the dead, descended from David. This is my gospel, for which I am suffering even to the point of being chained like a criminal. But God's Word is not chained! Therefore I endure everything for the sake of the elect, that they too may obtain the salvation that is in Christ Jesus, with eternal glory. Here is a trustworthy saying: if we died with him, we will also live with him, If we endure, we will also reign with him; if*

we disown him, he will also disown us; If we are faithless,
he will remain faithful, for he cannot disown himself.

(2 Timothy 2:8-13)

Endurance has both a vertical and horizontal reference. Paul endured hardship in order to please God and finish his God-assigned task. Paul had a proper vertical reference. Paul was motivated by the general call of 2 Corinthians 5:9, which says, *"So then whether at home or away from home, we make it our ambition to please Him."* Paul was rightfully goal-oriented, as every saint should be. For Paul, pleasing God meant ministering the good news to others—a proper horizontal reference. In verse 10, Paul said as much. He knew that God's eternal plan of salvation included those who had not yet heard the good news of salvation (Romans 10:13-17). Paul patterned his service after Jesus Christ (John 4:31-34). He had no qualms about God's eternal plan and God's means for completing it. This included election, which he did not consider a harsh teaching (verse 10). Because of it, Paul was assured that enduring to the end was God's means to His desired results. Therefore, Paul faithfully preached the gospel because God would provide fertile hearts.

Paul taught that endurance is a prerequisite for reigning in glory (Hebrews 12:1-4; Revelation 20:4). In 2 Timothy 2:8-9, Paul set forth at least two reasons for enduring. First, he remembered Jesus as the resurrected Lord and the supreme

Endurer. He is the One for whom Paul endured and suffered hardship. Paul's second reason for enduring was the fact that God's Word was not limited or made impotent because of what was happening to him (verse 9). Though the messenger may be imprisoned, God's Word never will be (Philippians 1:12-18; Isaiah 55:10-11).

Remembering who Jesus is and what He did is the key to endurance. It brings about an atmosphere of hope, joy, anticipation, and victory (Hebrews 12:1-3).

11.   Biblical endurance is *learned* and *maturing*:

> *You, however, know all about my teaching, my way of life, my purpose, faith, patience, love, endurance, persecutions, and sufferings – what kind of things happened to me at Antioch, Iconium, and Lystra, the persecutions I endured. Yet the Lord rescued me from all of them. In fact, everyone who wants to live a godly life in Christ Jesus will be persecuted.*
>
> (2 Timothy 3:10-12)

> *Teach the older men to be temperate, worthy of respect, self-controlled, and sound in faith, in love and in endurance.*
> (Titus 2:2)

Endurance was one aspect of Paul's life that Timothy was urged to follow. Paul had "one anothered" Timothy in a manner similar to the way Christ discipled the twelve (Acts 4:13;

Luke 6:40; Mark 3:14). Paul modeled endurance for Timothy, and Timothy is commended for his own endurance. Enduring biblically "feeds upon itself" and becomes a patterned way of life. Paul said that both hard times and God's deliverance from them is part of being a Christian (2 Timothy 3:12).

In Titus 2:2, Paul stated that older men must be taught various qualities, including endurance. They are to be learners. Paul knew that learning may be impeded because of failing bodies. He knew that all types of trouble occur in older age (loss of friends, spouse, or physical well-being, just to mention a few). But age alone and failing bodies are no excuse for failing to grow in the character of Christ.

The list of qualities given in verse 2 is not an exhaustive one. The teaching and developing of these qualities is needed in all age groups, irrespective of gender (older women: verse 3, and younger men: verse 6). Each age group has its own set of problems, but endurance is one of God's answers, no matter the saint's gender or age. Endurance, especially when it is hard to do, is a mark of maturity as a God-pleaser as well as one of the means for maturing.

CHAPTER 4

Jesus, the Model for Endurance

JESUS IS THE ULTIMATE ENDURER. But *what* did Jesus endure, and *how* did He endure? Consider Hebrews 12:2-3:

> *Looking off to Jesus, the Author and Completer of our faith, Who, for the joy that had been set before Him, endured the cross, despising the shame, and is seated at the right hand of God's throne. Consider him who endured such opposition from sinful men so that you will not grow weary and lose heart.*
>
> (Hebrews 12:2-3)

What Jesus Endured

These verses tell us Jesus endured the cross.[8] In one sense,

---

8   The time frame of "enduring the cross" is generally considered the time during Jesus' trial, scourging, mocking, and crucifixion. However, the

Jesus was free to exempt Himself from all trouble, including the cross. In another sense, Jesus was not and could not exempt Himself from cross-bearing. Pleasing His Father was Jesus' motivation for all of life, and He knew that the gateway to glory and to joy—both His and ours—was through the cross. He had no time to be distracted. He never took His eyes off His target: pleasing His Father, the joy set before Him, and a return to glory.

Hebrews 12:3 teaches that Jesus also endured opposition from sinners. While the work of Christ and the Cross focused on Christ's endurance in reference to the Father as an angry, just Judge, Christ also endured the wrath of bitter, envious sinners. Indeed, Jesus' entire life was one of affliction and opposition from family and friends as well as enemies. His parents didn't understand Him or the work He was sent to do (Luke 2:40-50). His disciples left Him even though they vowed they wouldn't. They failed to pray with Him when He told them to, and they didn't comprehend His teachings (Matthew 26:31-35, 40-46; John 14:8-11).

Consider the various groups who opposed Him. His chief opponents were the Pharisees and other teachers of the law.

---

phrase, "enduring the cross," should remind all believers of at least the toughness of Jesus' entire life (His race) and the manner in which He ran and completed His mission.

During and after His trial, and as He hung on the cross, Jesus was scorned and ridiculed by the Roman soldiers, thieves, and those passing by (Matthew 27:28-30,38-44). Imagine you, a sinner, standing up under such opposition. It is hard enough to endure such treatment from other sinners. Amazing as that may be, how unfathomable it is for the perfect, sinless Son of God!

Some may say that was His job. How incredibly self-serving, scandalous, and blasphemous to think of Christ, the Lord of lords and King of kings, as having a *job* to do. He was not our errand boy or "flunky." He came as part of the fulfillment of the Triune God's eternal decree of saving an undeserving, otherwise hell-bound people for Himself. He voluntarily condescended to become one of us, judicially bearing the guilt and condemnation in the believer's place.

How Jesus Endured

How was Jesus able to endure? Again we refer back to John 4:31-34, which gives the answer:

> *Meanwhile his disciples urged him, "Rabbi, eat something." But he said to them, "I have food to eat that you know nothing about." Then his disciples said to each other, "Could someone have brought him food?" "My food," said Jesus, "is to do the will of him who sent me and to finish his work."*

(John 4:31-34)

This passage documents the first "how" of Jesus' endurance. Jesus contrasted His source of satisfaction for life (which was pleasing His Father) with that of a more familiar source of pleasure: eating. Though His disciples experienced delight and pleasure from eating, Jesus pointed the disciples to something far superior: the satisfaction and contentment of pleasing God.

Jesus lived with an upward and eternal perspective, suprasensually, and wanting what the Father wanted. In contrast, the disciples, as fallen men, lived predominately according to their senses. They evaluated their circumstances by the "now:" by whatever seemed appropriate and relevant at that moment for relief and satisfaction (see the example of Esau in Genesis 25:27-34). Their focus was on the momentary, physical, personal, visible, created, finite, and material. In contrast, Jesus was motivated by His intimacy with the Father and desire to please Him. He processed life through His senses but evaluated that information based on His proper vertical reference to God and life. In that way, Jesus was able to please His Father in any and all circumstances. This enabled Him to endure the cross and sinful men, because He knew it was best for Him, the Father, and His people. Entrusting Himself fully to His Father, Jesus confidently stayed the course and ran the race set before Him, functioning as the Christian's Sinless Substitute. Trusting His Father meant denying Himself. How about you? To the degree that you depend on your own strength in any situation is the degree that you will fail to endure biblically.

Moreover, Jesus prepared Himself throughout His life for enduring the cross (Hebrews 2:10; 5:8).[9] He did this by dying to His own will and living to please His Father. Denying self was an integral part of His life. Briefly, denying self means actively, cognitively, and purposefully choosing to please God rather than self. In fact, Jesus' response to every event in His life pointed Him to the cross. He was resolute in His determination to accomplish His Father's goal—He lived suprasensually (Luke 9:51; John 4:31-34). Jesus did *more* than "hang in there." He joyfully remained true to His calling and thereby pleased God by doing His Father's will. In so doing, He accomplished God's plan, honored His Father, and ministered to others. The essence of biblical endurance is living as Jesus did. He made God's goal His goal, and He consistently kept His attention fixed on that goal. For Jesus, enduring the cross

9   Enduring the cross can be defined physically and spiritually. Physically, Jesus bore a wooden cross, and He bore the guilt and condemnation of sin and God's wrath that Christians deserve. Throughout His life, He prepared for the cross by denying Himself His wants and desires in favor of pleasing His Father. The road to glory for Jesus was by enduring the cross. There was no other way. The cross loomed large in Jesus' thinking, and enduring it was a divine necessity. Pleasing His Father trumped giving in to and satisfying His own desires and wants. In this sense, enduring the cross was a way of life for Him.

was not simply passive living and dying or just getting the job done by coping, accepting, getting through it, doing the best He could, pushing Himself, or dealing with the pain. Nor should it be for you!

Jesus also lived by priorities and schedules—another important point for biblical endurance. He knew that vengeance is God's and not His while He remained on earth as Savior. His role as Judge would wait until the proper time (John 5:22, 27; 9:39). Jesus entrusted Himself to His Father by remaining fixed on the goal set before Him. He remained on the cross as the perfect God-pleaser. Jesus did not use His authority and power inappropriately. Rather, Jesus came to save, not to judge (John 3:17; 12:47; Luke 19:10). Because Jesus faithfully endured, He accomplished His mission of saving a people and pleasing God. The two are inextricably linked. Jesus was committed to doing things God's way and remained true to the end. That is biblical endurance!

There are other examples in Scripture of Jesus' faithful endurance for our sake. His active ministry on the cross stands supreme. He remained on the cross in order to become sin and thereby save His people (2 Corinthians 5:21; Galatians 3:10-13; 1 Peter 3:18; John 17:1-5). He successfully ministered to one of the two thieves and to His own family (Luke 23:39-43; John 19:25-27). He prayed for His persecutors (Luke 23:34). What an amazing picture of faithful, hopeful, and successful godly endurance in the midst of such misery! Jesus' endurance is your model today. Biblical endurance will carry you through the valley of the shadow of death to your heavenly Father.

Peter cited the example of Jesus' faithful endurance when encouraging his people to endure during the pressure of Nero's persecutions.

> *He committed no sin nor was deceit found in His mouth. When they hurled their insults at him, he did not retaliate; when he suffered, he made no threats. Instead, he entrusted himself to him who does judge justly.   He himself bore our sins in His body on the tree, so that we might die to sins and live for righteousness; by his wounds you have been healed.*
>
> (1 Peter 2:22-24)

Jesus ran the race to glorify His Father. Pleasing His Father simplified life, and doing so was a great joy to Him, even though the cross itself was not. Jesus sweated blood over it (Luke 22:44). As we have discussed, suprasensual living wasn't possible only for Jesus. It was also true for the saints described in Hebrews 10 and 11, and can also be true for you, Christian.

Another Illustration of Suprasensual Living

Suprasensual living means that one evaluates life through the eyes of saving faith. This is part of the lesson of Psalm 73.

> *When I tried to understand all this, it was oppressive to me till I entered the sanctuary of God; then I understood their final destiny.*
>
> (Psalm 73:16-17)

There was a time in the psalmist's life when his focus was on the "now." He saw the wicked prospering and concluded that he had been shortchanged. Perhaps, faithfulness wasn't all that it was touted to be (verses 2-14). However, by God's grace, just in time, he had a radical reorientation (verses 16-19). Because it involved enduring biblically, he moved from an animal-like sensual approach to life to thinking supra-sensually (verses 16-19, 21).[10] He properly evaluated man's eternal destiny. As a result, he was satisfied and content in his circumstances. He called God the strength of his heart and his portion forever (verse 25-26).

The psalmist's mindset mirrors the way Jesus and the saints of old evaluated life. All of these faithful endurers looked forward to glory, thereby remaining firm and strong (enduring) in the present (1 John 3:1-3).

You may ask, "How is it that looking forward to glory fosters endurance, especially when I feel so bad and the end seems

---

10   My dog is a wonderful pet, but he is always the first to be fed, first to go outdoors, and never says thank you. Such it is with self-centered people – the "I wantsies" control their life. They live sensually.

so far off?" Everyone's race has a starting pointing and an end. Godly endurance enables you to know that you are in the race and to reach the finish line. In His Word, God tells you that the race is not endless, you have the capacity to respond in a Christlike manner, and you are not trapped (1 Corinthians 10:13 – see footnote #7). Because endurance is focused on and helps bring to mind God's grace, His promises, and your past deliverances, your progress will not be hindered. You run the race with God's goal and purpose in mind, which results in victory (Philippians 3:12-15; James 1:12).[11] The endurer is a winner, and winning is worth enduring. God rewards the winner. In fact, every Christian is, in one sense, a winner (1 Corinthians 1:30). His endurance is evidence of God's grace secured by Christ's endurance, and it is a testimony that he is God's child. That perspective also fosters endurance.

A Second How

In Hebrews 12:2 there is a second "how" of Jesus' endurance. He endured the cross by despising its shame. What does that phrase mean, and how did it help Jesus endure? Shame refers to the embarrassment, humiliation, disgrace, and utter

---

11   Victory is *being controlled* by biblical principles rather than one's own wants and desires. It means *pleasing* God by applying His truth in the situation rather than following self. And it is *using* the trouble as an opportunity to put self to death and to rely on the faithfulness of God.

disgust associated with crucifixion. In Roman society, the one crucified was considered an awful, horrible person. In a word, scum! Sinless Jesus considered as scum, cursed—think of it! God fully rejected Him, not for His own sins as many thought, but for those of *His* people (Deuteronomy 21:22-23; Galatians 3:13; Isaiah 53:4-6).

Yet, when Jesus looked at His humiliation, He despised (*kataphroneo*) it. Literally, the word means "to hold in contempt," "to think lightly of," or "to despise."[12] How does the word apply here? Jesus knew that He had to be considered a dreadfully wicked, guilty person by the Father and totally rejected by Him. He knew He had to go to hell on the cross. What a horrible thing for the holy, undefiled Jesus to contemplate! Yet, He could see what lay on the other side of the cross. His desire to please His Father was such a powerful incentive to complete His mission that He looked past His humiliation to glory. His goal was to please His Father, not to avoid humiliation!

Paul taught this same approach to life:

> *Your attitude should be the same as Christ Jesus: Who, being in very nature God, did not consider equality with God something to be grasped, but made Himself nothing, taking the very nature of a servant, being made in human*

---

12   Matthew 18:10; Romans 2:4; 1 Corinthians 11:22; 1 Timothy 4:10; 2 Peter 2:10; Matthew 6:24; Luke 16:13; 1 Timothy 6:2

likeness.   And being found in appearance as a man, he humbled himself and became obedient to death – even death on a cross!

(Philippians 2:5-8)

Jesus did not think being treated and worshipped as God was as important as pleasing His Father. He did not hold on to His glory while on earth. He did not live sensually by an "I deserve" or an entitlement mentality. Certainly, He deserved all that God deserves. Yet, He voluntarily honored His Father by forgoing the glory and praise due Him as Lord and King. He lived and died a cross-centered life. Jesus did not attempt to get even, become embittered, or keep score. He ministered.

The Christian follows Jesus' example as he pours contempt on all his pride. He endures by following Christ's Scripturally-sketched example. Like Christ, he, too, must set aside his wants and his rights. Self desire should conform to God's desire. Pleasing God and pleasing self are mutually exclusive. Therefore, the "I wantsies" must go, being replaced by biblical truth learned in a milieu of gratitude for who God is and what Christ has done for the believer.

A Third How

Besides His motivation to please the Father and despising the shame of the cross and sinners, a third *how* of Jesus' endurance is His eternal perspective: He looked forward to the reward of eternal joy. Jesus knew that in eternity past, God had determined unspeakable joy and grandeur for the winner. For Christ, He would be reunited with the Father in His rightful place of honor as the exalted, resurrected God-man before whom every knee would bow (Ephesians 1:20-23; Philippians 2:9-11). God's glorification was a most powerful impetus for Jesus to enduringly run the race. His joy and contentment was not based on circumstances, but on His intimate relationship with His Father. Jesus longed for heaven; therefore, He lived with the full knowledge of the Father's presence, power, promises, and provision, and in fulfillment of His perfect purpose and plan. So too should you.

For Christ, enduring the cross was a patterned way of life of denying self that culminated in completing His Father's work (see John 4:31-34). So it is for His saints today.[13] Moment by moment, He faithfully and hopefully endured as He cognitively and purposefully chose to please His Father.

---

13   Six times in the Gospels (Matthew 10:32-38; 16:24-25; Mark 8:34-35; Luke 9:23-24; 14:26-27; John 12:24-26), Jesus repeats His call for His disciples to deny self, take up the cross, and follow Him. In this way, they would non-redemptively imitate Christ. The cross is an instrument of death. Your cross is not someone or something but you desiring to put your wants and desires above pleasing God. As Jesus did, you must persevere in taking up your cross. Failure to do so carries a high cost: remaining in bondage; being shamed and renounced by Christ; and the destiny of being hell bound.

Such a choice was dictated by His intimate fellowship with His Father that gave Him an eternal perspective on life and enabled Him to focus on God's good, ultimate control.[14] As a result, His life and His work on the cross had meaning and purpose for Him and all believers.

Too often, professing Christians take a "what's in it for me?" approach to life. Let's be clear: God is the great Provider, and He graciously lavishes spiritual blessing upon spiritual blessing to every one of His children in this life in anticipation of the consummate wedding feast of the Lamb (Ephesians 1:3-14; Psalm 103:2-5; Revelation 19:6-8). However, as we have noted, a proper perspective on life means being heavenly minded (defined as a proper vertical focus; Christ-centered "eye-fixing;" and an eternal perspective). It is only then that you can be of earthly good. By earthly good, I mean being in the present

---

14   Jesus was the unique Son of God both eternally and as the incarnate God-man. Eternally, He and the Father are one (John 10:30) – unity yet diversity. In order to save a people for Himself (one God, three persons), Jesus became incarnate – He took the form of man (Philippians 2:5-8). On earth, Jesus was fully God and fully man without conversion, composition, or confusion of either nature. However, in His humanity, Jesus' Sonship is different from His eternal Sonship. Jesus related to the Father as the faithful, obedient Son with one mission: to please His Father. The double intimacy of Father-Son was an ever-present motivation for Jesus (John 16:31-32). In like manner, the believer is to imitate Christ because of his personal relationship with Him.

what God designed you to be in eternity past (Ephesians 1:4). Therefore, you must remember that pleasing God by becoming more like His Son is your greatest privilege and blessing this side of heaven. It is also the major means by which God is glorified (Romans 8:28-29). Your correct response to life and God's providence should be: "what is in it for God?" When He is glorified, you are storing up treasures in heaven (Matthew 6:19-24). God's glory and your benefit are inextricably linked. Final glorification comes in God's timing. All things come to pass for His honor and the benefit of His people as He brings many sons to glory (Hebrews 2:10). Godly endurance was one of God's means of glorification for Christ and the saints of old, and it is for His people today.

CHAPTER 5

Self-Pleasing: A Hindrance to Biblical Endurance

AS WE HAVE DISCUSSED, JESUS endured because of His relationship with His Father. Similarly, God's people endure biblically because of their union with Christ (see footnote 1). As a result, they successfully run the race of life with joy and contentment. Life is relational, and relationships matter (1 John 3:1-3; 1 Peter 1:8-10).

Enemy Number One: Self-pleasing

In Hebrews 12:4 (*In your struggles against sin, you have not resisted to the point of shedding your blood*), the author raised the stakes for godly enduring—his readers were struggling against sin. Their struggle was not in the abstract or against something or someone, but against their tendency to inordinately please self, which is a result of God's curse on sin (James 4:1). As discussed, this is manifested as sensual living. In contrast, the Christian has been changed and

radically reoriented with a new capacity to live suprasensually—pleasing God first and foremost (2 Corinthians
5:9, 14-17). Self-pleasing is the standard operating agenda
for every unbeliever and, too often, for the new creature
in Christ. This is because the believer still retains the habit
of self-devotion and self-worship learned so well from his
former membership in Satan's family and kingdom. The
believer still harbors the habits of self-pleasing and sensual
living manifested as the "I wantsies." This tendency can
be exposed any time, but it is especially during times of
trouble. Such was the case in the Hebrew congregation.
The real struggle was in their hearts.

The Christian's struggle is summarized in Joshua
24:15:

> *But if serving the Lord seems undesirable to you, then
> choose for yourself this day whom you will serve, whether
> the gods of your forefathers served beyond the River or the
> gods of the Amorites in whose land you are living. But as
> for me and my household, we will serve the Lord.*

It is captured by Paul in Galatians 5:16-18:

> *So I say live by the Spirit and you will not gratify the
> desires of the sinful nature. For the sinful nature desires
> what is contrary to the Spirit and the Spirit what is contrary
> to the sinful nature. They are in conflict with each other*

*so that you do not do what you want. But if you are led
by the Spirit, you are not under law.*

The two goals, pleasing self via the impact of previous
membership in Satan's family and kingdom and pleasing God
via the influence of the Holy Spirit, are mutually exclusive.
They are in competition. Godly endurance moves the person
away from self-pleasing and sensual living and toward pleasing
God and suprasensual living.

When trouble comes, biblical endurance enables you
to remain riveted on the finish line. Your running requires
Christlikeness. And as you run, you develop Christlikeness.
The two cannot be separated. Therefore, always consider
Christ. He faced pressures throughout His life of fighting the good fight and winning the race. Like us, He was
tempted to view pressure as something that He didn't
deserve (Matthew 4:1-11; Luke 4:1-13; Hebrews 4:14-
16).[15] Yet when He was squeezed 24/7, He pleased God
in thought, desire, and deed (John.4:31-34).

According to Hebrews 12:4, Jesus not only ran the race
by enduring the cross and bearing its shame, but by shedding

---

15   Hebrews 4:14-16 teaches, among other things, that Jesus understood
completely what the human condition was all about. Sinless Jesus completely
identified with mankind. He experienced the temptation of pleasing self in
contrast to pleasing God. His perfection was on the line every moment of
every day. Truly He endured and won!

His blood. Firmly committed to completing the race and winning the prize set before Him, Jesus stood strong in the midst of great distress. Jesus' endurance was supreme in accomplishing God's greatest gift—the salvation of His people as He pleased His Father.

The Active Side

There is an active side of biblical endurance: steady persistence in biblical well-doing in the face of good and hard times (Galatians 2:20; Philippians 4:13). This well-doing includes such activities as returning good for evil, reconciling one to another, submission to wrongly used but God-ordained authority, thankfulness in hard times, and loving the seemingly unlovable. (This list is obviously not exhaustive!)[16] Self-pleasing and living according to the "I wantsies" hinder the Christian from engaging in these activities.

In verse 3 of Hebrews 12 (*Consider him who endured such opposition from sinful men, so that you will not grow weary and lose heart*), the author used Jesus' endurance as a positive motiva-

---

16   The subject of returning good for evil is addressed in Romans 12:17-21, and reconciling one to another in passages such as Matthew 5:23-24, 7:1-6; Ephesians 4:31-32, Colossians 3:12-14. The subject of wrongly-used, God-ordained authority is addressed directly in 1 Peter 2:13-3:6 and indirectly in Ephesians 5:21-24 and Romans 13:1-7. Thankfulness is addressed in 1 Thessalonians 5:18, and loving the unlovable in Romans 5:6-10 and 1 John 4:7-12.

tion for his readers. In verses 1 and 2, the author also called his people "to stay in the race" and "run to win" as Jesus did. These two phrases are at the core of biblical endurance. Jesus endured because He knew who He was, and He lived out of that identity. The issue was never finding Himself or "getting in touch with his inner person." He did not function according to His own agenda, but according to His Father's will. Therefore, He vigorously pursued the goal of pleasing God by enduring the cross and the opposition of sinners (Hebrews 12:2-3).

In addition, the author of Hebrews called his readers to endurance with the words "don't give up." The word for "give up" implies faintheartedness, a "what's the use?" attitude, or a feeling of being overwhelmed and without resources.[17] "Not giving up," at least, means steadfastness and loyalty to a person and a task, and it is an inside-out activity. It is heart-generated and motivated. The call to not give up is hope-engendering.

Let's look at a couple whose life demonstrates active endurance. The "Donaldsons" own a business. They face mounting debt and bankruptcy because of fiduciary irresponsibility by at least one member of the corporation. What will they do? It would be easy to believe that they have been cheated

---

17   The word translated "give up" is *ekkakeo* and carries with it the idea of cowardice and losing courage: Luke 18:1; Hebrews 12:3,5; Galatians 6:9; Ephesians 3:13; 2 Thessalonians 3:13

and that God made a mistake. This couple finds themselves in severe straits and facing a theological cliff. How will they respond? Setting the course of pleasing God (2 Corinthians 5:9; John 4:31-34) and knowing that life is about becoming more like Christ (Romans 8:28-29), the Donaldsons set out to be good stewards of their time and energies by relying more and more on God and His Word. They find that there is light at the end of the tunnel because God is Light (John 8:12; 9:5; 1 John 1:5). Jesus has sailed these uncharted waters, and their relationship with Christ takes on a new meaning. He is their refuge and strength (Psalm 18:1-3; 46:1-2). Many twists and turns take place but in the end, saving the company and gaining financial security takes a back seat to honoring God. This comes about only as the couple endures biblically with the motivation of pleasing their God.

The Patient, Waiting Side

There is another side to biblical endurance: namely, aggressive, patient waiting.

Tom was physically down. His physical activity was significantly curtailed due to a failing body. I encouraged Tom to be an "aggressive waiter." Generally, waiting is considered passive and the person, physically inactive. Biblically, aggressive waiting means pursuing pleasing the Father in thought and desires, especially when one's own physical strength is waning. Increasing trust and dependence on a good God, an active prayer life, and a ministry to hurting people by phone or email (or texting) are only a few examples of aggressive waiting. Although my friend was limited physically, he was not trapped in his body or in the situation. Tom successfully endured by focusing on pleasing his God rather than getting what he wanted—relief.

Also consider "Bethany," young wife and mother of two, who was recently diagnosed with rheumatoid arthritis. She faces hurts, difficulty with the simple task of daily activities, both her own and her families, and the uncertainties of which—if any—treatment she should pursue. What does she do? How will she respond as a godly endurer? Remembering that she is to continue to think vertically, Bethany rests her hope not in a cure but in pleasing her God by being a good steward of her body (1 Corinthians 6:19-20). In this way, life is simplified and focused on how best to be a good steward. This is preparation for fighting the good fight, no matter what God in His providence brings in to a believer's life. She will remember, as will all godly endurers, that whatever happens is the best thing that absolutely can happen. That truth is because of the awesomeness of her/our God. His control is simply the best thing this side of heaven. Seeking to control by changing the situation and being cured will be not consume her. Simply pleasing God (Bethany's vertical reference) by good stewardship of her body, loving her husband, and mothering her children (her horizontal relationships) simplifies her life and unburdens her. Her body may be failing, but her God is not. Bethany draws enduring strength from that fact. Only a godly endurer can evaluate life from that perspective and live life to please God—not in spite of the situation, but using the situation as a tool to please God by becoming more like Christ.

Examples of aggressive waiting are given in the Psalms. In Psalm 37:7, aggressive waiting is described by the phrase "be still before the Lord." David was not to fret by becoming jealous when others, especially those who had wronged him and made life hard for him, seemed to be getting ahead. Instead, David engaged his mind in remembering his God and his own salvation. This motivated David to use the situation to please God when it was easy to please self. He did not "play God" by getting even and holding a grudge. In David's case, aggressive waiting meant keeping an eternal perspective on trouble, avoiding impulsive thinking and acting, and trusting more and more in his good God. And in Psalm 40:1, David waited patiently for the Lord to act by reflecting on his own past deliverances in times of trouble. He concentrated on the God of help and relished in his mind the results of God's enabling grace. As a result, his downtime physically was not polluted by fretting, bitterness, and anger.

A Word of Caution

Although every Christian's endurance is to be modeled after Christ's, man's endurance is not redemptive. There is a contrast between non-redemptive shedding of blood by God's people and Christ's shedding of His blood. Christ's endurance and the shedding of His blood led to the redemption of God's people. Your endurance doesn't accomplish God's saving purpose. It does accomplish God's purpose established in eternity past: for all believers to develop the character of Christ (Ephesians 1:4).

As we have discussed, the author of Hebrews had reminded his readers that they had endured in the past (Hebrews 10:32-34). More importantly, he instructed them that Jesus Christ had suffered to the point of shedding His blood (Hebrews 12:1-3). Not only that, scores of God's people who faithfully endured in serving God had shed their own blood (Hebrews 11). The present generation, however, had not (Hebrews 12:4). Endurance was needed for those times. Though endurance may lead you as well into and through physical suffering, Christ is worthy of that honor. That which He has prepared for you is worth faithfully enduring (Acts 5:40-41).

Consider Paul's words in 2 Corinthians 4:16-18:

> *Therefore we do not lose heart. Though outwardly we are wasting away, yet inwardly we are being renewed day by day. For our light and momentary troubles are achieving for us an eternal glory that far outweighs them all. So we*

fix our eyes not on what is seen, but what is unseen. For
what is seen is temporary but what is unseen is eternal.

He spoke of momentary, light afflictions in contrast to the eternal weight of glory that comes about by heart renewal. Endurance is a product of man's inward renewal—joy, hope, and thankfulness internally every day because of who he is and his ministry as a believer. Inner renewal requires and is demonstrated by godly endurance. Neither Paul nor the author of Hebrews minimized the Christian's hard times and bodily discomfort. Rather, they maximized the Savior, what the believer was in Christ, and God's saving and enabling grace. Thus, every saint was enabled to follow in Christ's footsteps. The same is true for God's people today.

Let me remind you of two important truths:

- Every saved person is united with Christ.
- Christ is the great High Priest who identifies with the believer in his difficulties (Hebrews 4:15). Christ experienced humanness in its entirety and yet did not sin. Christ knows what it means to want something other than the Father's desire and plan.

Therefore, Jesus, the Ultimate Endurer, gives purpose, meaning, and motivation for the Christian to endure victoriously.

CHAPTER 6

Summary and Conclusion

BIBLICAL ENDURANCE IS THE RESULT of a heart change. The reality of that change is demonstrated as the Christian develops more of the character of Christ. The enduring saint pleases God by *using* the situation as God's instrument for growth. He develops a growing capacity to remain firm and strong, especially when trouble abounds. The child of God consistently recalls who Christ is, what He has done, and who he is in Christ. As a result, he honors Christ when it is hard to do so and when it is easy to sin. The one who endures *uses* what he doesn't like and wishes were non-existent as a tool to become more like Christ. He does so by calling to mind and applying biblical principles in the midst of those times.

Endurance is also defined relationally, both vertically and horizontally. Because of the believer's personal relationship with God in Christ, he endures out of gratitude as he is empowered to please God. The pillars of biblical endurance are a proper vertical reference, an eternal perspective, suprasensual living, and trust in God's good control and providence. The Christian lives suprasensually with an eternal perspective of life through the eyes of saving faith and a growing trust in his trustworthy God. He sees the wonderful things that God has prepared for His people, including the privilege and blessing of becoming more like Christ. This heavenly-mindedness enables him to be of earthly good by putting off self-pleasing and putting on God-pleasing attitudes and actions. In this way, the Christian runs the race of life with endurance and gains the winner's wreath in heaven as well as a satisfied, contented life on earth.

A core aspect of biblical endurance is active faithfulness in using trouble to develop increasing Christlikeness. How about you? Are you convinced that biblical endurance is more than hanging in there? Do you believe endurance is the result of faithful commitment to knowing and doing God's will as taught in Scripture? Are you ready to exercise faith, hope, and love? Will you model your endurance after Jesus' example? You must pursue endurance. Don't lose sight of who God is, what you are in Christ, and the eternal joy set before you. It is what you have been set free to do (John 8:31–36). So, get busy enduring God's way!

CHAPTER 7

Homework

HERE ARE SEVERAL QUESTIONS TO help you consider how to endure God's way.

1. List the pressures and irritations in your life. Please be specific.

2. Write out your response to each of them, being as specific as you can. Include not only what you do in response, but also record your thoughts and desires.

3. Describe your endurance and the results.

4. Consider how your endurance looks in each of the situations on your list. Explains how it is:

   a. **Purposeful**: What is your purpose and motivation for enduring? Romans 5:1-5

   b. **Victoriously hopeful**: How is it so? Romans 8:23-25; 1 Thessalonians 1:3

   c. **Knowledgeable**: What are the facts on which your endurance is based? Romans 15:4

   d. **Intimately comforting**: In what ways has your

relationship with God in Christ impacted your endurance, and vice versa? 2 Corinthians 1:3-9

e. **Powerfully joyful**: How is your endurance joyful, and how has it helped you develop the fruit of the Spirit in terms of joy? Colossians 1:11

g. **Faithfully visible** and **worthy of praise**: What do others say about your endurance? What does it look like to them? 2 Thessalonians 1:4

h. **Inner-man** reality that is **learned**, **practiced**, and **maturing**: What did your endurance look like early in your situation, and how has it changed? 2 Thessalonians 3:5; 2 Timothy 3:10-12; Titus 2:2

i. **Pursued** and **developed**: In what ways are you pursuing and developing God's kind of endurance? 1 Timothy 6:11

j. **Faithful commitment**: Write your commitment to Jesus Christ and record how endurance fits into that picture. 2 Timothy 2:3

k. **Goal oriented**: What are you hoping to accomplish by enduring? 2 Timothy 2:8-13

5. What biblical truth do you need to focus on in order to help you **honor God** by **becoming more like Christ** in your situation instead of simply hanging in there, coping, tolerating it, or accepting it?

   a. How will endurance enable you to gain victory **in** the situation?

   b. How does victory look in your life when victory is defined as:

   1. Being **controlled** by biblical principles rather than your wants or the agony of the situation

   2. **Using** what you don't like and would rather leave or forget to become more like Christ.

   3. **Pleasing** God rather than pleasing self by seeking relief or bailing out

6. In what specific ways has endurance helped you get that victory? Please keep a weekly record of your progress.

7. Plan to record and review your progress at three, six, and twelve months. Discuss it with one of your church leaders or a spiritually-mature friend.

8. So, believer, have you experienced God's comfort? If you have, what has been the result?

APPENDIX

New Testament Words Relating to Endurance

THREE VERBS ARE TRANSLATED AS "to endure" (*upomeno, anechomai,* and *upophero*). One noun, *upomone,* is usually translated as "endurance." Other translations for the verbs include "to persevere," "to stand firm," and "to be patient."

I. *upomeno* **and** *upomone:*

    A. *Upomeno*: the verb is used seventeen times and is translated endure/endured, stand firm, persevere/persevered, stood ground, and stayed behind.

Matthew 10:22: All men will hate you because of me, but he who <u>stands</u> <u>firm</u> to the end will be saved.

Matthew 24:13: but he who <u>stands</u> <u>firm</u> to the end will be saved.

Mark 13:13: All men will hate you because of me, but he who <u>stands</u> <u>firm</u> to the end will be saved.

In these verses, biblical endurance is translated as "standing firm." Endurance doesn't save—it is one thing that saved people do. It is a testimony of God's work in their hearts. When persecution comes, God's call to the believer is to maintain loyalty to Him. Those who are loyal will enter into His glory.

Luke 2:43: After the Feast was over while his parents were returning home, he <u>stayed behind</u> in Jerusalem, but they were unaware of it.

Acts 17:14: The brothers immediately sent Paul to the coast, but Silas and Timothy <u>stayed at</u> Berea.

Romans 12:12: Be joyful in hope, <u>patient</u> in affliction, faithful in prayer.

Paul commands his readers to endure. The call to endure is hope-engendering because God gives no commands for which His saints have not been equipped. Biblical endurance is a mark of the believer.

1 Corinthians 13:7: It always protects, always trusts, always hopes, always <u>perseveres</u>.

In the "love" chapter, Paul gives one characteristic of biblical love: it is continual and unbreakable. It requires biblical endurance. Non-enduring love is not love.

2 Timothy 2:10, 12:

Therefore I <u>endure</u> everything for the sake of the elect that they too may obtain the salvation that is in Christ Jesus with eternal glory.

If we <u>endure,</u> we will also reign with him; if we disown him, he will also disown us.

These verses teach that biblical endurance is purposeful and goal-oriented. It accomplishes something. Failure to endure biblically results in being disowned—in the end, rejected by God.

Hebrews 10:32: Remember those earlier days after you had received the light when you <u>stood your ground</u> in a great contest in the face of suffering.

The writer reminds his readers of their prior endurance as motivation for continued endurance.

Hebrews 12:2-3, 7:

v.2: Let us fix our eyes on Jesus, the Author and Perfecter of our faith, who for the joy set before him <u>endured</u> the cross, scorning its shame, and sat down at the right hand of the throne of God.

v.3: Consider him who <u>endured</u> such opposition from sinful men so that you will not grow weary and lose heart.

v.7: <u>Endure</u> hardships as discipline; God is treating you as sons. For what son is not disciplined by his father?

These verses teach that Jesus is our model for biblical endurance. Since Jesus endured, and Christians are joined to Christ (united to Him, in fellowship with Him), saints of all ages are to follow Christ's example and will follow His example.

Christians practice hope-based endurance by fixing their eyes on Jesus who has endured, is in glory, and is calling them home. Biblical eye-fixing enables them to think about their hard times as teaching tools. God's purpose for hard times is *not* necessarily for the believer to seek relief, but for the believer to *use* those hard times to develop

Christlikeness by enduring God's way.

James 1:12: Blessed is the man who <u>perseveres</u> under trial because when he has *stood the test,* he will receive the crown that God has promised to those who love him.

According to James "standing the test" is the result of enduring biblically. James is calling his people to complete the race as victors. The way of victory is to continue applying biblical principles to all of life with the motive of pleasing God out of gratitude for what Christ has done and is doing seated at the Father's right hand.

James 5:11: As you know, we consider blessed those who have <u>persevered</u>. You have heard of Job's perseverance and have seen what the Lord finally brought about. The Lord is full of mercy and compassion.

God is merciful and blesses those who endure His way.

1 Peter 2:20: But how is it to your credit if you receive a beating for doing wrong and <u>endure</u> it? But if you suffer for doing good and you <u>endure</u> it, this is commendable before God.

Peter, writing to his congregation that would soon experience horrible times, gives God's view of their situation. Peter asks: what benefit is it to you, and how does it glorify God, when you endure the consequences for your own wrong doing? Peter's and God's answer: it doesn't! However, when hard times are not the result of your own sin and you endure, you please God, which is the believer's greatest privilege and goal this side of heaven.

B. *Upomone*: the noun occurs some thirty-one times and is

usually translated as endurance or perseverance.

Luke 8:15: But the seed on good soil stands for those with a noble and good heart who hear the word, retain it, and by <u>preserving</u> produce a crop.

The parable of the Sower is about fruit-bearing—good and bad. Only the biblical endurer produces the good fruit that God expects and deserves.

Luke 21:19: By <u>standing firm,</u> you will gain life. See Matthew 24:13 and Mark 13:13.

Romans 2:6-8:

v.6: God will give to each person what he has done.

v.7: To those who by <u>persistence</u> in doing good seek glory, honor, and immortality, he will give eternal life.

v.8: But for those who are self-seeking and who reject the truth and follow evil, there will be wrath and anger.

In verse 7, the key word is <u>endurance,</u> which leads to continuing in doing good. Doing good is contrasted with self-seeking in verse 8. Biblical endurance looks away from self to God and His purpose in the situation. The biblical endurer *uses* the situation to develop Christlikeness.

Romans 5:3-5:

v.3: Not only so, but we also rejoice in our sufferings, because we know that our suffering produces <u>perseverance,</u>

v.4: <u>perseverance</u>, character; and character, hope.

v.5: And hope does not disappoint us, because God has poured out his love into our hearts by the Holy Spirit, whom he has given us.

The word translated as "sufferings" is a general word for trouble (*thlipsis*). How does trouble produce perseverance? It doesn't. Trouble itself has no innate power; it is neutral. But it is the context for the believer to express his heart motivation. It is only when he rightly responds to trouble that good things come (remember that good is defined as God's way: becoming more like Christ (Romans 8:28-29; Ephesians 1:4). The biblical endurer knows (verses 3 and 4) that God is good and purposeful. Therefore, the Christian experiences the joy and benefit of pleasing God by enduring *in* the trouble.

Romans 8:24-25:

v.24: For in this hope we were saved. But hope that is seen is no hope at all. Who hopes for what he already has?

v.25: But if we hope for what we do not yet have, we wait for it patiently.

These verses give a clear definition of hope and link enduring God's way to it. The biblical endurer is confident because he relies on the promises of God. Without biblical hope, the Christian has no eternal perspective, and he will not endure. Expectant, confident hope is based on God, who is infinitely trustworthy, and on His promises, which are being fulfilled. The Christian lives suprasensually, and as he does, God is honored and the Christian endures.

Romans 15:4-6:

v.4: For everything that was written in the past was written to teach us so that through the <u>endurance</u> and encouragement of the Scripture we might have hope.

v.5: May the God who gives <u>endurance</u> and encouragement give you a spirit of unity among yourselves as you follow Christ Jesus,

v.6: so that with one heart and mouth you may glorify the God and Father of our Lord Jesus Christ.

Hope is so important to the believer that God has lavishly provided it. He has gifted believers with endurance and encouragement that comes through the Scriptures. In them, God proclaims His promises and His trustworthiness, thereby encouraging His people to become more like Christ. Biblical endurance is one way to grab hold of God's promises and act on the reality of a never-changing, good God. The end result is the honor and glory of God.

2 Corinthians 1:6: If we are distressed, it is for your comfort and salvation; if we are comforted, it is for your comfort, which produces in you <u>patient endurance</u> of the same sufferings that we suffer.

You became the most comforted person when God saved you. God sends trouble to enable you to experience His comfort and help. In trouble, you learn something about God and yourself. This verse teaches that God's comfort and help produce endurance. You are to endure *in* trouble, in part, so that you can comfort others.

2 Corinthians 6:4: Rather as servants of God we commend ourselves in every way with great <u>endurance</u>; in troubles, hardships, and distresses;

In verses 4-9, Paul highlights his troubles. In contrast to false teachers, his commission is from God, and he functions as a servant of God.

That is evident because of his great endurance in all of life especially in seemingly continuous troubles. Enduring biblically was a mark of his apostleship, and by it he was following Christ's example.

2 Corinthians 12:12: The things that mark an apostle—signs, wonders, and miracles—were done among you with great <u>perseverance</u>.

Paul was diligent in presenting Christ and in protecting the message and the One who sent him. His endurance was a mark of his apostleship. Paul took God's work seriously, which was a testimony to God's work in him. So too should believers of all ages.

Colossians 1:9-12:

v.9: For this reason, since the day we heard about you, we have not stopped praying for you and asking God to fill you with the knowledge of his will through all spiritual wisdom and understanding,

v.10: And we pray this in order that you may live a life worthy of the Lord and may please him in every way: bearing fruit in every good work, growing in the knowledge of God,

v.11: being strengthened with all power according to his glorious might so that you may have great <u>endurance</u> and patience, and joyfully

v.12: giving thanks to the Father, who has qualified you to share in the inheritance of the saints in the kingdom of light.

Paul's prayer teaches, among other truths, that biblical endurance and joyful thanksgiving *in* or *out* of trouble, guided by the Holy Spirit, is the way to the heavenly inheritance designated and preserved by God for Christians (also see 1 Peter 1:3-5).

1 Thessalonians 1:3: We continually remember before our God and Father your work produced by faith, your labor prompted by love, and your <u>endurance</u> inspired by hope in the Lord Jesus Christ.

Paul encourages fellow believers by calling attention to the fruit of God's work in them. One of those fruits is biblical endurance. Paul teaches that biblical endurance is to be seen and remembered.

2 Thessalonians 1:3-4:

v.3: We ought always to thank God for you, brothers, and rightly so, because your faith is growing more and more, and the love every one of you has for each other is increasing.

v.4: Therefore, among God's churches we boast about your <u>perseverance</u> and faith in all the persecution and trials you are enduring.

Biblical endurance is focused, faithful, visible, and purposeful. It was an encouragement to Paul and should be for other Christians. Evidence of God's grace, especially in the face of trouble, is truly a blessing and a source of joy.

2 Thessalonians 3:5: May the Lord direct your hearts into God's love and Christ's <u>perseverance</u>.

Christ's perseverance is described in Hebrews 12:1-3. He endured the cross and the opposition of sinful men. He is our model. Endurance is a matter of the heart, and the heart of the matter is the heart. The issue for every Christian is enduring or not enduring biblically.

1 Timothy 6:11: But you, man of God, flee from all this and pursue righteousness, godliness, faith, love, <u>endurance</u>, and gentleness.

Biblical endurance is to be pursued diligently and vigorously, which is evidence of and the result of God's grace and the working of the Holy Spirit in the believer.

2 Timothy 3:10: You, however, know all about my teaching, my way of life, my purpose, faith, patience, love, <u>endurance</u>,

Titus 2:2: Teach the older men to be temperate, worthy of respect, self-controlled, and sound in faith, in love, and in <u>endurance</u>.

Paul teaches that biblical endurances are to be taught and learned.

Hebrews 10:36: You need <u>to persevere</u> so that when you have done the will of God, you will receive what he has promised.

Hebrews 12:1: Therefore, since we are surrounded by a great cloud of witnesses, let us throw off everything that hinders and the sin that easily entangles and let us run with <u>perseverance</u> the race marked out for us.

The writer of Hebrews pointed to an essential ingredient of life. It was biblical endurance. He was not making a suggestion but stating a fact. Biblical endurance was, and is, required to run the race and finish the course as a victor.

James 1:2-4:

v.2: Consider it pure joy, my brothers, for various kinds of trials,

v.3: because you know that the testing of your faith develops <u>perseverance</u>.

v.4: <u>Perseverance</u> must finish its work so that you may be mature and complete, not lacking anything.

James 5:11: As you know, we consider blessed those who have persevered. You have heard of Job's <u>perseverance</u> and have seen what the Lord has finally brought about. The Lord is full of compassion and mercy.

James opens his epistle with a remarkable concept: his people needed to have their faith refined. Since faith is a gift from God, the gift was not the problem; it was the exercise of it (see Matthew 6:30; 8:26; 14:30; 16:8). James is addressing the issue of practical and functional atheism. Biblical endurance is faith in action, working through love: God's love of the believer and the believer's love of God. Since every believer has much growing to do, faith must be strengthened. God's chosen method is by testing. The testing of one's faith is required for growth in spiritual maturity. The latter occurs when the believer responds to his God-ordained situation by enduring God's way. As James closes his epistle (5:11), he reminds his congregation of the exhortation found in James 1:12: Christians are winners through biblical endurance.

2 Peter 1:5-6:

v.5: For this very reason, make every effort to add to your faith goodness; and to goodness, knowledge;

v.6: and to knowledge, self-control; and to self-control, perseverance; and to perseverance, godliness;

Biblical endurance is required to bear the fruit that God expects (2 Peter 1:8-11; Galatians 5:22-23; Ephesians 1:4; 2:10).

Revelation: 1:9; 2:2-3, 19; 3:10; 13:10; 14:12:

1:9: I, John, your brother and companion in the suffering and kingdom and patient endurance that are ours in Jesus, was on the island of

Patmos because of the word of God and the testimony of Jesus.

v.2: I know your deeds, your hard work and your <u>perseverance</u>. I know that you can't tolerate wicked men, that you have tested those who claim to be apostles but are not, and have found them false.

v.3: You have <u>persevered</u> and have endured hardships for my name, and have not grown weary.

v.19: I know your deeds, your love and faith, your service and <u>perseverance</u>, and that you are doing more than you did at first.

3:10: Since you have kept my command to <u>endure patiently</u>, I will also keep you from the hour of trial that is going to come upon the whole world to test those who live on earth.

13:10: If anyone is to go into captivity, into captivity he will go. If anyone is to be killed by the sword, with the sword he will be killed. This calls for <u>patient endurance</u> and faithfulness on the part of the saints.

14:12: This calls for <u>patient endurance</u> on the part of the saints who obey God's commandments and remain faithful to Jesus.

Trouble is the lot of every believer. And biblical endurance is his privilege (1:9). The book of Revelation is about the end times, either for Jerusalem (which occurred in 70 AD due to their failure to repent) or the last days that we are living in now, or both. There is no question that horrible persecution loomed large for unrepentant Israel. Also, the book of Revelation is a message of encouragement and exhortation. In it, Christ is presented as the Ultimate Overcomer (1:8, 17-18; 21:6-7; 22:12-13). Therefore, the martyrs and soon-to-be martyrs are viewed as overcomers through biblical endurance.

II. *Upophero*: this verb is used three times. It is translated "stand up under," "bear up," and "to endure."

1 Corinthians 10:13: No temptation has seized you except what is common to man. And God is faithful; he will not let you be tempted beyond what you can bear. But when you are tempted, he will also provide a way out so that you can <u>stand up under</u> it.

This hope verse contains at least four promises: 1. Nothing that befalls you is unique. Someone has had a similar experience or the similar pressure of responding in a self-pleasing manner (see Hebrews 4:15); 2. God is faithful; He is trustworthy and worthy of your trust; 3. In His providence, God will not exceed your spiritual capability for responding in a God-honoring manner; 4. Often, God's way out is to stay *in* the problem His way for His glory.

2 Timothy 3:11: persecutions, sufferings—what kinds of things happened to me in Antioch, Iconium, and Lystra, the persecutions that I <u>endured</u>. Yet the Lord rescued me from all of them.

Paul is passing the baton to Timothy and in the process gives him a charge. Timothy would face hard times (such as described in 2 Timothy 3:12). Problems would force him to reevaluate life, self, and God.

Especially in hard times, you will come to rely more and more on the Rescuer God who abundantly supplies grace and power so that you will endure biblically.

1 Peter 2:19: For it is commendable if a man <u>bears up</u> under the pain of unjust suffering because he is conscious of God.

Peter draws a distinction between sufferings because your action (or inaction) warrants punishment or because you, acting in the name of Christ for His glory, are wrongly punished. In the latter case, biblical endurance takes center stage and is needed to respond in a God-honoring manner.

III. *Anechomai*: this verb appears fifteen times. It is translated "to hold in or back," "to put up with," "bear with," "listen to," and "doing that."

Matthew 17:17 (parallel verses: **Mark 9:19; Luke 9:41**): "O unbelieving and perverse generation," Jesus replied, "how long shall I stay with you? How long shall I put up with you? Bring the boy to me."

A man approached Jesus and told Him that his demon-possessed son wasn't healed by Jesus' disciples. He asked if Jesus would heal him. Jesus responded by asking how long He should "put up" with this group of people that included His own disciples. Before any answer could be given, He commanded them to bring the boy to Him, and He healed him.

The unbelieving generation contrasted with His own confident trust in His heavenly Father. Motivated by the desire to please His Father, Jesus put up with people and His distressing circumstances. Their hard hearts were no reason for Jesus to turn away from them and His mission. And thank God that Jesus endured!

Acts 18:14: Just as Paul was about to speak, Gallio said to the Jews, "If you Jews were making a complaint about some misdemeanor or serious crime, it would be reasonable for me to listen to you.

Here Luke pictures "putting up with" as "listening to" and a most reasonable thing to do.

1 Corinthians 4:12: We work hard with our own hands. When we are cursed, we bless; when we are persecuted, we <u>endure</u> it;

Similar to the teaching in Matthew 5:43-48; Romans 12:17-21; and 1 Peter 2:19-23, Paul gives the biblical response to being sinned against—it is to endure by relying on God and His promises.

2 Corinthians 11:1, 4, 19-20:

v.1: I hope you will <u>put up with</u> a little of my foolishness; but you are already <u>doing that</u>;

v.4: For if someone comes to you and preaches a Jesus other than the Jesus we preached, or if you receive a different spirit from the one you received, or a different gospel from the one you accepted, you <u>put up with</u> it easily enough.

v.19: You gladly <u>put up with</u> fools since you are so wise;

v.20: In fact, you even <u>put up with</u> anyone who enslaves you or exploits you or takes advantage of you or pushes himself forward or slaps you in the face.

In verses 1-15 of chapter 11, Paul is speaking of his ministry in contrast to the ministry of the false apostles who were teaching a false gospel. In verse 1, Paul writes that the Corinthians are putting up with him. As godly endurers, they had heard and responded properly to the gospel. However, in verse 4, their "putting up with" was actually undiscerning tolerance that gave the false teachers a foothold in the Corinthian Church.

In verses 19-20, Paul continues to rebuke the Corinthians for their non-biblical endurance. Tolerating someone or something is not godly endurance. Their approach to the false teachers had serious repercussions.

Ephesians 4:1-3:

v.1: So as a prisoner of the Lord, then, I urge you to walk in a manner worthy of the calling that you received.

v.2: Be complete humble, and gentle; be patient, <u>bearing with</u> one another in love.

v.3: Make every effort to keep the unity of the Spirit through the bond of peace.

In the first three chapters of the book of Ephesians, Paul lays out non-negotiable doctrinal truths, and, beginning in chapter 4, he begins to focus on right application. He transitions from doctrine to application by urging God's people to have a certain mindset. From this mindset will flow certain behaviors, including putting up with one another in love. Here, *anechomai* has the idea of restraining yourself in order to walk and talk as brothers and sisters in Christ. In these verses, the motive for bearing with is to keep and guard the bond of peace. Where there is strife, there is self-grasping and self-exaltation and no peace (James 3:13-18). When individuals attempt to be number one, they are competing with God. The result is chaos and disunity.

Colossians 3:12-13:

v.12: So then as God's chosen people, holy and dear, clothe yourself with compassion, kindness, humility, gentleness, and patience.

v.13: <u>bearing with</u> each other and forgiving whatever grievances you may have against one another. Forgive as the Lord forgave you.

Paul has zeroed in on interpersonal relationships. However, the vertical reference to life controlled their horizontal relationships. He knew that people operate simultaneously in both dimensions. Bearing with includes having a willingness to forgive. Judgmentalism, fault-finding, and blaming others are ways of not bearing with. For the church's sake, God's honor, and the believer's good, the Christ-like characteristics listed in verse 12 must replace self-centeredness. When believers function as God-pleasers, the peace of God is ruling in the heart of individuals and in Christ's church.

In Ephesians 4:1-3 and in Colossians 3:12-14, Paul calls the members of both congregations to follow Jesus' model. The Christian is the most "put up with" person—God saved him when, humanly speaking, there was no reason to do so. Since that is the case, he is to imitate God by loving the unlovable (Romans 5:6-10).

2 Thessalonians 1:4: Therefore among God's churches we boast about your perseverance and faith in all the persecutions and trials you are <u>enduring</u>.

Paul was amazed at God's work in the saints at Thessalonica. He was encouraged, and he encouraged them to continue as faithful, biblical endurers.

2 Timothy 4:3: For the time will come when men <u>will</u> not <u>put up</u> with sound doctrine. Instead, to suit their own desires, they will gather around them a great number of teachers to say what their itching ears want to hear.

Paul tells Timothy that he will face opposition to sound (literally, doctrine that is healthy and hygienic) doctrine. The reason: people are easily motivated by the "I wantsies"—sensual living. Self-pleasers will enlist teachers who serve them. Both the listeners and false teachers are not biblical endurers.

Hebrews 13:22: Brothers, I urge you to <u>bear with</u> my word of exhortation, for I have written you only a short letter.

The writer of Hebrews closes his letter with an exhortation to pay attention to and heed his words. As in Acts 18:14, "putting up with" includes listening *and* doing (Matthew 7:21-27).

For more information about
Dr. Jim Halla
&

Endurance
please visit:

www.JimHalla.com
JimHalla@gmail.com
facebook.com/JimHalla

....

For more information about
AMBASSADOR INTERNATIONAL
please visit:

www.ambassador-international.com
@AmbassadorIntl
www.facebook.com/AmbassadorIntl